Culture and Child Protection

Reflexive Responses

Marie Connolly, Yvonne Crichton-Hill and Tony Ward

Jessica Kingsley Publishers
London and Philadelphia

First published in 2006
by Jessica Kingsley Publishers
116 Pentonville Road
London N1 9JB, UK
and
400 Market Street, Suite 400
Philadelphia, PA 19106, USA

www.jkp.com

Library of Congress Cataloging in Publication Data
Connolly, Marie.
 Culture and child protection : reflexive responses / Marie Connolly, Yvonne Crichton-Hill and Tony Ward.
  p. cm.
 Includes bibliographical references and index.
 ISBN-13: 978-1-84310-270-0 (pbk. : alk. paper)
 ISBN-10: 1-84310-270-6 (pbk. : alk. paper) 1. Children--Services for. 2. Social work with children. 3. Culture. I. Crichton-Hill, Yvonne. II. Ward, Tony, 1954 Mar. 17- III. Title.
 HV713.C665 2006
 362.76--dc22
                                                         2005022366

British Library Cataloguing in Publication Data
A CIP catalogue record for this book is available from the British Library

ISBN-13: 978 184310 270 0
ISBN-10: 184310 270 6

Printed and bound in Great Britain by
Athenaeum Press, Gateshead, Tyne and Wear

For George, John and Claire

Feelings tell us where we are and what is happening to us. They are also the traces of where we have been and of what has happened to us there. If we advance gropingly we do so with the aid of our feelings. Whether we are moving through the worlds of perception or through the infinitely rich symbolic worlds of meaning collectively created by ourselves – our cultures – we must have systems of navigation in place if we are not to lose our way and become disoriented or lost.

Ciarrãn Benson,
The cultural psychology of self (2001, p.103)

Acknowledgements

This book is based on the knowledge we have gained through working with people; the children, families and offenders whose lives and experiences have directly informed the ideas presented in these chapters. We have learned much from them. We would like to thank our colleagues who have also contributed to the development of this book. Ideas are generated through conversations, sometimes casual, sometimes as a result of like-minded people getting together to work through tricky issues of child care and protection. We have appreciated their input and in particular we are grateful to our colleagues who work in policy and practice. They keep us up to date with their important work. Our thanks to Elizabeth Rathgen whose keen editorial eye has once again been invaluable. Thanks also to the Department of Child, Youth and Family, Victoria University of Wellington, and the University of Canterbury for their continued support. We would also like to thank our partners and families who have kept our homes warm while we sat in front of our computers for just one more hour...

Contents

Preface

Some years ago an academic colleague undertook research with senior social work students within our university – the University of Canterbury.[1] She looked at the ways in which students appreciated difference and cultural diversity and how this appreciation influenced their practice. She taped supervision sessions between students and their supervisors and looked at how issues of difference and diversity were addressed in the context of the supervision sessions. Her findings astonished us. She found significant gaps in the students, appreciation of cultural issues in practice and, indeed, a surprising inability on their part to articulate cross-cultural concepts in the context of practical realities. Further, the supervisors also struggled to unmask subtle – and not so subtle – themes of oppression in supervision.

Perhaps not surprisingly we were dismayed by these findings. The students had been undergoing social work training for some years and their courses provided extensive exposure to critical theory and cross-cultural course content. The supervisors were professionally qualified and had been trained in supervision. Why then did the tapes reveal so little evidence of anti-oppressive thinking in reported practice? As we reflected on this we were even more disconcerted to realise that this particular cohort of students were well able to articulate complex postmodernist notions of identity and difference in the classroom in ways that reflected a sophisticated knowledge of critical theory and practice. It seemed they understood oppression in the abstract but had not made meaningful personal connections with the people they were seeing. We wondered why the learning from their training was not translating into real world practice. Why were they able to articulate this appreciation of culture and difference theoretically but barely at all in the context of field practice? These questions have been fundamental to the writing of this book. They have caused us to explore the nature of the way we

---

1   The research was undertaken by Dr Jane Maidment who is now Associate Professor of Social Work at University of Central Queensland.

think about culture and oppression and they have caused us to think about what impacts on our capacity to understand the world outside ourselves. This book then is about cultural thinking and how it influences the way we respond in practice.

We have taken a broad stroke in exploring culture and cultural thinking. While we pay particular attention to ethnicity, we also discuss the ways in which cultural thinking more generally shapes the way we think, feel and act. For example, we look at childhood cultures, family cultures and cultures of abuse and offending. We also look at theoretical cultures since they are so influential to the way in which we behave as helping professionals. Any set of explanatory propositions, whether they are professionally based or are derived from our personal and family experiences, is considered here under the broad umbrella of *cultural thinking*. Cultural thinking shapes our investigations, our interpretations and our responses. As such it is of extreme importance if we are to understand better the people we work with and how we think about them and work with them. Sometimes cultural thinking supports helpful professional practice, sometimes it can be a hindrance.

We begin the book by looking at how cultural thinking develops and how it informs the way we understand the world around us. We explore the reasons why it is so difficult to accurately perceive the world of another, and why it is so easy to impose our views on others even when we believe we are being culturally responsive. Chapter 2 then looks at what we can do about that. Because cultural thinking is so critical in shaping practice we look carefully at the ways in which our personal and professional selves impact on the work. While personal experience has long been seen as influential in practice, less attention has been paid to how theoretical and philosophical cultures have driven the work and how they too have the potential to become automated responses – even when they may not fit well with the people we work with.

Chapter 3, completing the first half of the book, takes us to the broader organisational environment of child protection and the issues relating to developing culturally responsive practice within this environment. Administrative approaches to the work have tended to dominate practice in recent years and here we explore culturally different ways of thinking about how we do the work.

The second half of the book then goes on to explore the nature of cultural practice. We begin this set of chapters by looking at children's cultures. Although child care and protection work is by nature child-focused, practice continues to largely reflect adult-to-adult processes where decisions are made for children in their best interests. In the past two decades writers have challenged the way in which children have been invisible in research and practice, and in Chapter 4 we look particularly at the 'new social studies of childhood' and the way in which they support a more child-centred philosophy. Keen to introduce children's voices into the book, we have reviewed research undertaken directly with children. Their reflections upon their experience suggest that we would do well to listen more carefully to children if we want to develop culturally responsive services for them.

Families nurture our ideas and beliefs and influence what we think and do. They have their own communication patterns and organisational systems that help family members make sense of their world. Understanding family cultures is important if child care and protection workers are to harness family strengths and foster positive change. In Chapter 5 we talk about the potential to enhance practice and build culturally supportive services for families. However, even with the best intentions, family work is a complex endeavour made particularly challenging in the context of cultural diversity. It is easy for a worker to lose their way and so we present a simple model of supervision that can help workers navigate cultural territories.

When protecting children it is not possible to separate the components of the abuse matrix – the child, the protectors and the abusers. Practitioners across the sphere of child abuse work need to know how different helping systems are intended to protect children from harm. This means also knowing and understanding cultures of offending. We therefore turn our thoughts to abuse and offending in Chapter 6. Our experience of working with men who sexually offend suggests that while they often struggle to find non-offending pathways, they are as keen as everyone else to have a rewarding and 'good life'. Tapping into this strength-based potential provides an opportunity to develop cultures of positive change through services that focus on compassion, respect and the building of well-being.

Finally, in Chapter 7, we construct an holistic theoretical perspective that blends ideas and theories that we have discussed throughout the book. We see theories as cultural resources that help us to assess and intervene in situations of child abuse. It seems to us that issues of theory development and appraisal have been largely neglected within the area of child care and protection, with most current interest centring on assessing risk and measuring outcomes. In developing the culturally reflexive model that we describe in Chapter 7, we are exploring ways in which cultural thinking and theory can be knitted together to provide more culturally responsive practices.

The ideas presented in this book reflect our own struggles with the complexities of culture, human behaviour and practice. We have been concerned by the refractory nature of practices that fail to respond effectively to cultural imperatives. While theories and tools can give us a sense of familiarity and certainty that enables us to confront the distress of children and families, they can sometimes take on a life of their own. We can continue to cling to them even when they no longer have currency or they fail to resonate with the people we work with. Children and families have changing needs and to be helpful our practice needs to change and develop alongside them. This is one of the important challenges of child care and protection work. It is the challenge of culturally responsive practice.

Part One

Culture and
child protection work

Chapter 1

Culture, the client and the practitioner in child protection work

A greying man and a young woman are dancing. He is English, and he says to her, 'You have such a lovely face; it's a pity about your accent.' Her face is half Japanese and half European, perhaps German or Slav or French...she has to explain it. Her accent is American. She does not think that he is right to be sorry for her; on the contrary, she feels she was born in the right century because she belongs entirely neither to the East nor to the West.

Theodore Zeldin
An intimate history of humanity (1994, p.43)

What we think about people culturally different from ourselves – whether they are beautiful or odd, whether we agree or disagree with their beliefs – influences both how we interpret what they do and how we respond to them. These cultural interpretations emerge from, and are deeply connected to, the ways in which we experience and interpret our own lives within our own world. And although we may talk a good deal about culture and how powerful it is in shaping the way humans think about the world, when it comes down to actually trying to understand the world of another, we can be taken by surprise at how difficult it can be and how discordant it feels measured against the security of our own beliefs.

Although culture is a fundamental component of human existence, it has been described as a complex and elusive concept (O'Hagan, 2001). Cultures comprise subtleties and peculiarities that are often taken for granted by cultural group members and which may not be understood by those outside the group. Understanding the meaning of culture, and our own cultural limitations, is critically important to the development of culturally responsive work in child care and protection. It is not surprising, therefore, that this is where we begin this book. Understanding culture facilitates our understanding of how others interpret their social world. Because our behaviours generally correspond with our interpretations of our social world, working *with* cultural contexts is more likely to result in successful practice outcomes than is fighting against them. Whenever a practitioner is working with diversity – whether it relates to ethnicity, sexuality, religiosity, disability or across class structures – an appreciation of the dynamics of culture will foster greater recognition and responsiveness to elements of prejudice, discrimination and oppression in practice.

Conceptualising culture

According to Eagleton (2001, p.1), 'culture is said to be one of the two or three most complex words in the English language....'. It has been described as 'a difficult concept to grasp' (Diller, 1999, p.48), and 'the most inclusive term but also the most general' (Hays, 2001, p.10). In addition, meanings change over time, place and context (Eisenhart, 2001). In early times, *culture* was connected with the cultivation of crops and with agriculture. It was also associated with spiritual worship, and this component of its use led to the development of the term 'cult' (Smith, 2001). Elements of the original definition remain, and when people today speak of their 'culture' they often refer to their land of origin (O'Hagan, 2001).

Between the sixteenth and nineteenth centuries culture was associated with human improvement and refinement. The development of notions concerning appropriate etiquette and protocol informed beliefs about who could be identified as civilised and who could be identified as uncivilised. Social hierarchies depended on wealth. Daniel Defoe's early eighteenth-century classification of English society makes this clear (Salmond, 2003, pp.11–12):

1. The Great, who live profusely.
2. The Rich, who live very plentifully.
3. The Middle Sort, who live well.
4. The Working Trades, who labour hard, but feel no Want.
5. The Country People, Farmers etc; who fare indifferently.

6. The Poor, that fare hard.

7. The Miserable, that really pinch and suffer Want.

On a broader scale, societies were categorised as either civilised or 'barbaric'. This highlights a period of time where 'new reflection about differences among human populations had been prompted by European exploration and conquest across the globe' (Spillman, 2002, p.2). The catalyst for this reflection was the Industrial Revolution, when a series of inventions revolutionised productive capacity and heralded the progression of humankind, first in Great Britain and later in Europe and the United States. This led to the classification of cultures according to advances made in the West, thereby positioning European cultures as superlative and the benchmark by which all other cultures were judged.

Towards the end of the nineteenth century, anthropologists elaborated on earlier understandings of 'culture'. Culture became linked with traditions and experiences of everyday life as anthropologists attempted to study human behaviour systematically. By encountering different cultures, anthropologists were able to compare differences between the cultures of many different groups of people. Early anthropological notions identified social life within a culture as primarily homogeneous and static.

Williams (1976) postulates that the term 'culture' in contemporary times reflects the changes in description historically. Thus 'culture' has broadly three connotations:

- Culture as the process of intellectual and aesthetic development.

- Culture as intellectual and artistic activity (for example, film, art, theatre).

- Culture as a way of life of people (including values and norms).

It is the third connotation of culture that is of most interest to child protection practitioners, and within it there are at least some dimensions that have been generally agreed upon. Essentially, culture is understood to relate to some shared elements which connect people in a common way of experiencing and seeing the world. These perceptions of the world guide day-to-day living, influence how decisions are made and by whom, and determine what is perceived to be appropriate and inappropriate behaviour within any given context. As Kim (2001, p.48) suggests, 'culture is imprinted on each individual as a pattern of perceptions, attitudes, and behaviors that is accepted and expected by others in a given society below the level of conscious thought'.

Because culture exists below the level of consciousness, and is so deeply embedded it escapes everyday thought, the term is difficult to quantify. Ambiguousness in meaning is further complicated by a lack of clarity as to the group referred to when employing the term 'culture'. While there have been numerous attempts at theorising culture as a way of life for a group of people, much recent work has advocated the view that culture is synonymous with ethnicity and, to a lesser extent, race.

Ethnicity can be defined as the term given to a group of people who share a common ancestry which includes common cultural practices (McLennan, Ryan and Spoonley, 2004). This may imply a common biological ancestry; however, according to Hays (2001, p.12) the 'most important aspects in terms of individual and group identity are those which are socially constructed'. Important to the understanding of ethnicity is the potential for diversity within an ethnic group: 'ethnicity is a malleable and often contested subjectivity...and there is often more than one way of expressing or practising a particular ethnicity' (Spoonley, 1994, p.84).

Race, on the other hand, refers to a way of classifying people on the basis of geography and physical characteristics which was first developed in the seventeenth century (Spickard, 1992). As with all classification systems, race is primarily concerned with inclusion and exclusion; the definition of one in opposition to the other. Furthermore, race has been described as a dangerous concept, particularly when physical characteristics are linked with intellectual capacity and the proposition that these aspects are measurable (Montague, 1997). Ultimately, this results in a hierarchical system where some sectors in society are perceived as inferior to others. Preferring the term *ethnic group*, Montagu (1997, pp.2–3) further suggests that the concept of 'race' is in fact a myth, as the biological differences between people 'are superficial, and far fewer in number than the traits we have in common...these differences have come about as a result of the long isolation of such populations during which the physical differences have evolved'.

Despite these differences in meaning, the terms 'ethnicity', 'race' and 'culture' are often spoken of interchangeably. However, an even broader interpretation of culture is indicated when people use different ways to describe their cultural identity, including aspects of age, gender, social status, religion, language, sexual orientation and disability (Dean, 2001; Fellin, 2000; Pederson, 1991).

Cultural identity

In addition to notions of race, ethnicity and culture, the concept of *identity* has been popularised by the discipline of psychology. In particular, two theories of identity have held centre stage: identity theory and social identity theory. Both theories suggest that the process of self-classification contributes to the formation of an identity.

The hypothesis behind *social identity theory* is that people identify with particular social groups and this connection is important to the development of self-esteem (Tajfel, 1978). The tendency is for members of social groups to compare themselves with other groups resulting in notions of 'in-group' (where it is desired to be) and 'out-group' (where it is not desired to be). A person's self-esteem is enhanced by viewing the in-group in a positive light, while the out-group is viewed negatively (Stets and Burke, 2000). Conversely, identity theory emphasises that the self is a reflection of society. Therefore, as society is complex, multifaceted and organised, so too is the self. The way in which the self is organised, according to identity theory, is through the hierarchical organisation of roles (e.g. student, nurse, social worker and patient). Surrounding the self-categorised roles are defined expectations or standards of behaviour that people attempt to achieve. The role hierarchy exists as some roles will be more important to us than others (identity theorists term this *identity salience*). Identity salience is thought to have a direct influence on behaviour and influences our relationships and our perceptions of ourselves and of others. While there are distinctions between these two theories, Stets and Burke (2000) suggest that social identity and identity theory actually have more in common than in opposition with each other. In particular, they emphasise that a more comprehensive theory of identity would recognise the importance of both group and role categorisation in the formation of identity.

Cultural identity is often considered to be commensurate with national identity; however, while national identity has connotations of national pride and geographical location, it is culture that provides the ordering of social relationships and the structuring of ritual. There are limitations with the concept of cultural identity and writers have both challenged and supported aspects of this. Kim (1994) suggests that common notions of cultural identity inflate the worthiness, exclusivity, uniformity and permanence of cultural identity. *Worthiness* relates to the suggestion that the linkage between positive self-concept (identity) and cultural identity is beyond question. While Kim (1994) questions this, Mossakowski (2003) advocates that mental well-being is, indeed, protected by strong identification with an ethnic group. *Exclusivity* relates to the perception that cultural identity means belonging to one cultural group. However, as noted above, the dimensions that comprise one's cultural identity are many and varied. *Uniformity* is linked to the notion that cultural groups are homogeneous. This is far from accurate, and Kim (1994) suggests that a negative consequence of this idea is the likely promulgation of stereotypical generalisations. Finally, the notion of *permanence* suggests that cultural identity is static, fixed and unchanging rather than being flexible and adaptive.

The idea of cultural homogeneity has been powerfully enduring over time. Such a notion supports the development of 'one-size-fits-all' responses that may be economically efficient but are unlikely to meet diverse needs within ethnic groupings. If one considers that culture is learned and transferred from generation to generation, it is also inevitably person-specific and shaped by one's personal and social context. For example, siblings within a migrant family may be seen as being the same by people from the outside, but may experience very different cultural contexts within their adopted country environment – and may respond very differently to their experiences. Each will have been influenced by their particular social context, including those aspects of context that maintain oppression, prejudice and discrimination.

Oppression, stereotypes, prejudice and discrimination

Oppression, prejudice and discrimination are intimately linked. *Oppression* refers to relationships of dominance expressed across a range of contexts: personal, institutional, cultural and social. The key point here is that oppression is *relational*. As Dominelli (2002, p.9) aptly puts it, 'oppression takes place in the social arena in the form of interactions between people'. Oppression is not a static concept, but is dynamic and multifaceted. When thinking of relationships of dominance and subordination, one may be inclined to think of two groups: those who dominate, and those who are dominated. This fails to recognise the complexity of role and identity. Since a person's culture is informed by a number of identities, some aspects of that identity may experience the role of oppressor and other aspects the role of oppressed (Dominelli, 2002; Mullaly, 2002). For example, a child protection worker within a statutory agency may be viewed by a family as an oppressor – someone who is dominant and overbearing and able to wield immense power over them. That same child protection worker may feel powerless within their agency, unable to work in the way they want, oppressed by the long hours and high workloads. If the worker belongs to an ethnic minority group, they may also experience oppression within their professional and personal lives. Recognising that individuals identify with multiple cultures has led to an acknowledgement that there are multiple ways in which people may experience oppression (Williams, 2004).

According to Pharr (1988), relationships of domination are maintained through the dominant groups' classification of themselves as 'the norm'. Typically, the norm holds political, social, economic and linguistic power, described by Morrison Van Voorhis (1998) as 'privilege'. Any group that does not subscribe to the same values, beliefs and protocols is classified as 'other'. Within this context of cultural domination, the achievements of the 'other' remain invisible. As Pharr (1988, p.58) puts it:

> By those identified as the Norm, the Other is unknown, difficult to comprehend, whereas the Other always knows and understands those who hold power; one has to in order to survive…the Other's existence, everyday life, achievements are kept unknown through invisibility…when there is false information, distortion of events, through selective presentation or the re-writing of history, we see only the negative aspects or failures of a particular group.

Invisibility of the 'other' is maintained by stereotypes, prejudice and discrimination.

People have a tendency 'to categorize in an attempt to sort reality into neat and orderly arrangements' (Blumenfeld and Raymond, 2000, p.21). As society becomes more diverse, there is greater opportunity for prejudice and discrimination to develop, both of which are encouraged by stereotyping. Clients of child welfare services may have been negatively affected by oppression, prejudice and discrimination. Understanding how these concepts interrelate is important if the worker is to avoid further marginalisation of the families with whom they work. This possibility is enhanced structurally by child protection systems that are guided by the values of the dominant culture expressed through legislation, policy and practice frameworks. Sometimes systemic oppression occurs imperceptibly in the busy day-to-day practice of child care and protection work. A fuller understanding of the dynamics of prejudice and discrimination can help a worker limit the potential for children and families to be even further marginalised by the systems that are designed to support them.

Our ability and tendency to categorise forms the basis of prejudice and discrimination. This ability, termed *social categorisation* (Stangor, 2000), occurs when we identify someone on the basis of appearance or role as belonging to a particular group. Immediately we make this association, we build our thoughts and feelings about this group. This is a naturally occurring behaviour and Stangor (2000) suggests that we would find it difficult to survive without it. We categorise people just as we categorise other aspects of our lives. However, social categorisation is enabled by *stereotypes* that are defined as judgements and beliefs attributed as characteristic of all members of a particular group. This is where the difficulty lies, giving rise to a rudimentary and potentially flawed understanding of the group in question.

In sum, stereotypes are category-based beliefs about people. *Prejudice* is an attitude, an 'adverse opinion or belief without just ground or before acquiring sufficient knowledge' (Blumenfeld and Raymond, 2000, p.22) that occurs toward a group or a member of a group. *Discrimination* is the behavioural manifestation of prejudice and essentially refers to behaviours which exclude others. While it may appear reasonable to suggest that stereotypes cause prejudice which then results in discriminatory behaviour, the connections between the three concepts are more complex. Both prejudice and discrimination take on many forms, and may be overt or subtle. Furthermore, whether prejudice (attitude) is converted to discrimination (behaviour) is dependent on motivation and on whether the situational context is one where the expression of prejudice is accepted and/or expected (Schneider, 2004). The interplay between prejudice, discrimination and oppression can readily find its way into child protection practice and family violence.

Consider a situation where protective services have been involved with a migrant family and the children in this family have been witnessing domestic violence. The child protection practitioner was aware that the mother was regularly exposed to severe beatings by the father and decided to involve a victim support service worker in her discussions with the mother. The discussions focused on helping the mother to understand how the violence was harmful, not only to herself but also to her children. The mother agreed to leave the family home with the children, and the victim support worker assisted the mother to find accommodation and financial assistance.

The move was extremely difficult for the mother who had never lived independently with her children and had only recently moved to the country. She also had trouble speaking English and was not yet connected to other people from her country of origin. After a few weeks, feeling alone and isolated, the mother returned with her children to the family home.

Concerned about her safety, the child protection practitioner contacted victim support to arrange a follow-up visit. On receiving the call, the victim support worker expressed a reluctance to be involved with this family. She had found the mother difficult because of her limited ability to speak English, and was somewhat resentful that she had put all this work into the family to no avail. She commented that there were plenty of English-speaking families that needed help, and that she thought it a poor use of resources and time to work with people from these countries who always went back for their 'daily bashing'. Protective services later took action to protect the children, as it was considered that their safety could not be secured at home.

This situation illustrates the ways in which clients can be affected by complex layers of prejudice and discrimination. Prejudicial views about women as victims of domestic violence overlap with views about migrants and expectations of how they should adapt to their new adopted country. The potential for discriminatory practice in these situations is high, not only in terms of the outcome of the intervention, but also because of the cultural messages of support or lack of support that the family receives throughout the process.

Culture and child care and protection

Culture influences child protection practice in two key ways. First, considerations of abusive and protective behaviour towards children are culturally bound. Second, culture informs the range of professional responses to abuse. How abuse is defined critically informs how and when a worker intervenes. The debate surrounding the smacking of children illustrates this connection.

Some people define smacking a child as abuse, while others consider it an appropriate means by which a parent can control a child's behaviour. How you define it influences what you think should be done about it. Workers who see smacking as abusive are more likely to initiate action to prevent it. Those who believe smacking is a form of discipline are less likely to take action. These ideas are culturally constructed and rest at the heart of child protection practice. Cultural values and beliefs are often most strongly reflected through child-rearing practices, as Munro (2002, p.50) states:

> Definitions of abuse ... embody beliefs about what child rearing behaviour is unacceptable or dangerous and values about people: the relative rights of adults and children, the relative value of males and females. Hence, there is considerable variation over time and between cultures in what is deemed abusive.

There is no universality regarding child-rearing standards nor the definition of child abuse (Korbin, 1991). Incorporating a cultural perspective presents something of a dilemma. On the one hand, lack of cultural perspective in definition promotes the worker's own cultural values and world-view as the guiding force in determining whether abuse has occurred. Absence of a cultural perspective also promotes some dominant cultural values over others. Conversely, when definitions of child abuse are totally guided by cultural concerns, the outcome may result in some children receiving a lesser standard of care or protection (Korbin, 1991). Studies have tended to focus on speculating that some cultures are prone to abusive behaviour rather than trying to understand how child maltreatment is affected by culture (Korbin, 2002). Given cultural subtleties, it is important to be able to differentiate between child-rearing practices that enhance children's well-being, and those that are potentially harmful.

Korbin (1991) identifies three aspects which may be useful in developing culturally responsive definitions of child maltreatment:

- *Acknowledgement of cultural differences in child-rearing practices.* Customs considered acceptable and appropriate in one culture may be considered abusive by those outside the culture. For example, is it appropriate to place a leash around a toddler when in a public place, or is it akin to treating a child like an animal? If this was a culturally specific practice, how would it influence thinking about child-rearing practices within this particular cultural group?

- *Deviations from the culturally appropriate child-rearing practices of any specific cultural group are considered by that cultural group to be abusive.* Korbin (1991, p.69) suggests that 'it is at this level that child maltreatment is most legitimately identified across cultural contexts'.

- *Circumstances exist where societal harm undermines children's well-being beyond the control of the parent.* For example, poverty is understood to be beyond parental control and therefore distinct from child-rearing practices.

Korbin argues that difficulties with defining child maltreatment have arisen from a failure to differentiate between these three levels.

In relation to how culture informs professional responses to child mal-treatment, Korbin (2002) further suggests that incorporating a cultural com-ponent in child care and protection prevention and intervention is a necessity rather than an optional extra. Current knowledge of child protection work has traditionally been based on research and clinical experience in Western nations. Given the increasingly diverse nature of society, the need for more culturally specific research and clinical understanding is imperative. This is particularly important given the growing acknowledgement of disparities in health care and other social indicators, suggesting that minority groups are likely to suffer more serious consequences as a result of child maltreatment (Korbin, 2002). More than ever before, child protection practitioners need to develop proficiency and understanding in working with a diverse range of cultures.

Cultural relationships: the client and the practitioner

A recent study on the disproportionate representation of ethnic minority children and families in the child protection system found a number of factors influencing overrepresentation (Chibnall *et al.*, 2003). Poverty was found to be important, the result being minority families were more likely to be involved in the public health system and therefore more visible to a wide range of professionals. Increased media attention to child abuse and neglect nationwide created a climate of concern for local community and agency administration. This resulted in greater pressure being placed on workers to substantiate a higher number of cases. As Chibnall et al. (2003, p.25) suggest, for those agencies based in African-American communities 'substantiating more cases means substantiating more cases involving African-American children and families'. However, of particular importance to this discussion was the finding that worker bias was a factor given for overrepresentation. The study concluded that this bias interfered with good decision-making and arose from a lack of understanding of the cultural practices of minority populations. This has the potential to maintain power discrepancies and as Hays (2001, p.33) writes, 'when bias is reinforced by powerful groups and social structures, the results are systems of privilege and oppression'. This is acutely important to the nature of the client/worker relationship.

The ability to be culturally responsive in practice goes beyond skill proficiency and sensitivity to cultural diversity alone (Yee Lee, 2003). Three key areas have been identified for the development of culturally responsive practice: attitude, knowledge and skills (Diller, 2004, Ka Tat Tsang and George, 1998; Lum, 2003).

Practitioner cultural attitude

Fundamental to culturally responsive practice in child protection is the depth of understanding the practitioner has of their own cultural identity and attitude. This entails developing an awareness of those aspects of their individual cultural identity that are both conscious and below the level of conscious thought – a process we will discuss further in Chapter 2. It is a process that Weedon (1987) identifies as 'subjectivity', that is, one's sense of self and how one understands one's relationship to the world. An examination of one's personal subjectivity necessitates an understanding of the values and norms that inform one's own world-view, including the socio-political history that supports that world-view. Integrating this understanding with knowledge of the impact of oppression, prejudice and discrimination on self-concept and how this influences cultural biases and stereotypes is an important source of self-knowledge. Such understanding is not only essential for culturally responsive practice, but is necessary for the practitioner to know the limits of their ability.

McPhatter (1997) suggests that this process of awareness development needs to consist of engagement with various cultural communities over a sustained period of time. Brief, intermittent approaches are not regarded as helpful (Diller, 2004; McPhatter, 1997). Rather, genuine efforts to build relationships with a variety of cultural communities increase the likelihood of positive consequences for child protection work. Families involved in the child protection system have their own cultural identity, and it is important for child protection practitioners to consider the picture they have of the family in its identification with particular cultural communities. As Walmsley (2004, p.70) notes:

> Practitioners' thinking about the community is influenced by the community's openness to collaboration, the availability of support services, the distance the practitioner needs to travel to reach the community, the practitioner's vision of child protection practice and the practitioner's relationship history with the community.

Child protection workers have an opportunity to develop relationships with diverse cultural communities so that these communities become partners and protectors in the child protection relationship. Conversely, child protection workers are equally able to hold adversarial relationships with cultural communities. In these situations, there is potential for the worker to support oppressive, prejudicial and discriminatory responses based on their limited knowledge of their client's cultural community. It is clear that stereotypes about cultural communities are often derived from lack of understanding, contact or a narrow focus of information.

Practitioner knowledge

Writers have suggested that there is disparity in the social work literature as to the categories of knowledge necessary for effective culturally responsive practice (Ka Tat Tsang and George, 1998). Moreover, much of the available literature appears to focus on acquiring knowledge of the range of skills required for cultural encounters. This approach has been conceptualised in the child protection literature as the *cultural literacy approach* (Dyche and Zayas, 1995). The crux of this approach is culture-specific information and practice responses most often categorised under broad ethnic group categories.

There are a number of limitations to this approach. First, it would be impossible for workers to have an in-depth knowledge about all the client cultures that connect with protective services. Second, the approach has a tendency to create overgeneralisations of cultural groups. Third, the approach in effect places a worker in the position of 'expert' despite the likelihood of them being in a position of cultural naivety.

While it is recognised that some specific cultural knowledge is important, writers have argued that it needs to be extended to include an emphasis on knowledge of system context, including knowledge about 'current structural inequalities, racial politics, histories of colonization, slavery, and other forms of oppression' (Ka Tat Tsang and George, 1998, p.85). This understanding is considered to be fundamental to cultural competence (Lum, 2003).

Practitioner skills

The areas of attitude and knowledge need to be translated into a repertoire of professional behaviours (Ka Tat Tsang and George, 1998; Lum, 2003). Lum categorises three types of skills: process skills, conceptualisation skills and personalisation skills, all of which need to be developed within the context of cultural knowledge. *Process skills* relate to the child protection social work process and include an ability to engage with clients, develop rapport, and conclude client/practitioner relationships using a range of micro skills. *Conceptualisation skills* are essentially analytical skills that enable workers to analyse a case, uncover themes in client messages and plan effective assessment and intervention strategies. These are essential skills when practitioners may have a raft of information – sometimes conflicting information – about the circumstances surrounding a child's care and safety. Finally, *personalisation skills* involve the ability to have empathy with the client, and to be open and respectful of client challenges without taking a defensive stance.

The three components of practitioner attitude and cultural identity, knowledge and skills should be viewed as interwoven and dependent on each other. This interwoven skill base takes time to develop requiring also a desire and commitment to learn. As McPhatter (1997, p.260) quite rightly notes:

> The first step toward achieving cultural competence is understanding and accepting the reality that openness to long-term, ongoing, and persistent development is required. As in all professional development there is no ideal completion…any serious initiative to work effectively with diverse client populations begins with this premise.

Child protection practice is fraught with difficulties. When culture is added to the mix, the difficulty of the work intensifies and becomes infinitely more complex. A lack of knowledge about cultural contexts, identity and disadvantage has the potential to seriously compromise a worker's ability to understand the issues facing families who abuse and neglect their children. Lack of cultural knowledge also impacts on the worker's capacity to access culturally responsive solutions. Like any learning process, developing culturally responsive practice takes concerted effort – 'good will is not enough' (Narayan, 1999, p.244). Perhaps hardest of all, it takes commitment to interrogate our own beliefs about cultural ascendancy and our own powers to impose our views on others.

Chapter 2

Culturally reflexive responses in abuse work

Having looked broadly at culture and child protection, we now look specifically at how cultural thinking both shapes and impacts on practice.[1] Child protection work exists within a complex environment that is strongly influenced by individual, professional and societal values. The child protection area is infused with strong emotions, values and beliefs around what constitutes abuse and how society 'should' protect children. Professional decision-making and practice inevitably occurs in the midst of these contested discourses. Inevitably, cross-cultural dynamics add to this complex mix.

Cultural diversity enriches practice as we learn from people's experiences and interpretations of their worlds. Pasts are culturally saturated, and it is easy to lose one's way when navigating the cultural landscape of another. Indeed, one's own cultural landscape is often so complexly embedded that its impact on our beliefs and understandings can sometimes be underestimated. Being so familiar, our own way of thinking and our own way of life can so easily seem 'simply human' to us: 'it is other people who are ethnic, idiosyncratic, culturally

---

1   This chapter is partly drawn from 'Cultural components of practice: Reflexive responses' by M. Connolly in T. Ward, D. R. Laws and S. M. Hudson (2003) *Sexual deviance: Issues and controversies* (Chapter 6), used with permission.

peculiar. In a similar way, one's own views are reasonable, while other people are extremist' (Eagleton, 2000, pp.26–7).

In this chapter we are particularly concerned with the way in which cultural thinking impacts on and contributes to practice. Whether a worker is working with men who sexually offend or with young people who act abusively, with children who have been abused or with women who have experienced family violence, an examination of the cultural self as an integral and active agent within this complex matrix can help us to navigate through the inevitable meaning barriers that exist when working cross-culturally. Meaning barriers exist between all people, and when there are cultural differences, meaning barriers can be even more acute. What happens between the worker and the client, and between the client, the client system and the worker, can be, of course, a dynamic force for change. The way in which the worker system and the client system intersect and engage in a process of reciprocal exchanges will, by necessity, influence client outcomes. Because of the familiarity of cultural thinking, we may underestimate just how much impact this has on client outcomes. Nevertheless, it is inevitably a component within the worker/client relationship, and it is important to understand how cultural contexts influence the direction of the work and the process of change.

Cultural knowledge within the practice setting

There is a tendency when thinking about culture to assume that if a worker learns about a client's culture – what Spradley (1994) refers to as *explicit cultural knowledge* – then they will have some kind of template for working within that culture. Explicit cultural knowledge includes the specifics around what to do when you enter the cultural world of another – cultural protocols, customs, rituals, and the like. However, as Berlin (2002, p.144) quite rightly notes:

> classifying people on the basis of group membership only gives us the illusion that we are being culturally sensitive, when, in fact, we are failing to look beyond easy characterizations for the particular and specific ways that *this* person is understanding, feeling, and acting.

While it is clearly important to avoid cultural transgression by becoming familiar with cultural aspects of the populations we work with, it is perhaps even more important to understand the nature of tacit cultural knowledge:

Tacit cultural knowledge...is often outside our awareness... How we respond within a situation will depend on the complex transmission of cultural signs and symbols. Our responses to these are often automatic and deeply embedded. The values underpinning our cultural views also reflect ways of thinking that may have been handed down over generations. Such cultural views influence our behaviour. (Connolly, 2001, p.24)

It is often our tacit cultural understandings that get us into trouble cross-culturally. Because tacit cultural knowledge is frequently outside our awareness, we neglect to see its impact and the way in which it influences the process of the work. According to Giddens (1984, p.282), 'the knowledgeability of human actors is always bounded on the one hand by the unconscious and on the other by unacknowledged conditions/unintended consequences of action'. Having explicit cultural knowledge does not necessarily protect a worker from being influenced by tacit cultural assumptions. Indeed, as noted earlier, such knowledge can give the illusion of cultural sensitivity while cross-cultural misunderstandings remain camouflaged. Being aware of the potential impact of one's own cultural thinking helps to avoid unintended consequences that may emerge from client/worker misunderstandings. Hence, cultural self-knowledge can be seen as the first step toward understanding the components of cultural practice.

Locations of cultural thinking

Culturally reflexive reactions can be identified in a number of locations. The *personal self* provides one location for reflexive reactions. Using Bourdieu's (1990) notion of personal identity and its impact on the construction of the object, the personal self can be seen to be critically influenced by a range of differing factors: the person's gender, class, nationality, race, education, religion, family background, experience, and so forth. Of course, the notion that these factors have the potential to powerfully influence professional behaviour is not new. Indeed, most practice texts will refer to this potential in some way (see for example, Connolly, 1999; Fook, 2002; Taylor and White, 2000). The capacity for personal belief systems to provide a buffering effect for workers in times of stress has also been identified as a source of strength (Bell, 2003). Nevertheless, the power of the personal self to exert undue influence continues to pose problems for practice. A basic human instinct is to maintain the stability of our world – including the ideas that support that world. Ultimately, this can affect our capacity to 'change lens' and see and understand better the world of another:

> our own world suddenly becomes self-evident, so unproblematically 'the way it is,' that the other's world can seem blatantly incoherent... Instead of inviting mutual inquiry into our ways of world making, we defend our world, even impose it on others. (McKee, 2003, p.3)

It could be argued that one of the more dramatic examples of the personal imposition of power is to be found in the work of Sigmund Freud. In 1897, when Freud was in the midst of a personal crisis – and ten years before he published his theory of the Oedipus Complex – he wrote to an intimate confidant:

> Being totally honest with oneself is a good exercise. A single idea of general value dawned on me. I have found, in my case...the phenomenon of being in love with my mother and jealous of my father, and I now consider it a universal event in early childhood... (the Greek legend seizes upon a compulsion which everyone recognizes because he senses its existence within himself) Everyone in the audience was once a budding Oedipus in fantasy and each recoils in horror from the dream fulfilment here transplanted into reality, with the full quantity of repression which separates his infantile state from his present one. (Toews, 1998, p.65)

Clearly Freud saw these personal insights into his own childhood as holding true for the rest of humanity. Essentially, however, it may more accurately reflect an entirely egocentric discovery that later became the basis from which Freud convinced the scientific community of a universal process. Despite having no clinical evidence to the contrary, he quickly and completely abandoned his earlier 'seduction theory' in favour of this new idea that was so potently reinforced within his own experience. Later, he was to claim 'the beginning of religion, morals, society and art all converge on the Oedipus complex' (Toews, 1998, p.66).

Few have had the power to the influence the world's thinking in the way of Freud and, clearly, this is an extreme example of how the personal self can have the capacity to influence theory and outcomes. Nevertheless, reflexivity functions as an unavoidable but normal process and will inevitably influence how we operate as workers, clinicians, researchers or theorists, for good or ill.

The scope for cultural reflexivity is broad. As Nussbaum (2001, p.171) notes, 'culture only exists in the histories of individuals...individuals vary greatly, and...the existence of diverse personal patterns creates spaces for

Similar theoretical orientations can be found in child protection work. Internationally, service delivery systems respond to a unique set of cultural conditions that reflect societal expectations about how the state and the community should intervene in the lives of children and families. According to Hetherington (2002), three important factors influence the development and functioning of child welfare systems: structures, professional ideology and culture. Structural systems influence the way in which interventions occur and support the thinking that rests behind them. For example, law that enshrines family participation in child welfare decision-making inevitably shapes the way we think about family involvement and the rights of the family to participate in matters that concern them (Connolly, 1999). Professional ideologies also guide practice and influence workers in their decision-making. Hetherington (2002) notes that while organisational structures, resources and law provide the framework for child protection practice, actual decision-making is often based on professional knowledge and theory. Systems of child care and protection are also influenced by the culture of the society within which they exist: 'Culture influences and expresses expectations of the various roles that should be played by the state, the family, and by the community in relation to the child' (Hetherington, 2002, p.14).

Not surprisingly, therefore, cultural differences in philosophical orientation have critically influenced the development of child care and protection service delivery. Examining systems in other countries, writers have argued that it is possible to broadly differentiate child welfare responses into two welfare orientations: child protection and family support (Gilbert, 1997; Hetherington, 2002). Countries that have a child protection focus (for example, England, Canada, US and Australia) have been found to be more legalistic in approach with a strong emphasis on investigative procedures and applying resources at the 'front end' of the child protection process. By comparison, countries in continental west Europe (for example, Belgium, Sweden, France and Germany) have adopted more of a family support orientation. These countries have been found to place a greater emphasis on prevention within a broader system of universal welfare (Connolly, 2004). It is not the purpose of this chapter to argue the strengths and weaknesses of either response, but, rather, to highlight how cultural and philosophical orientation can critically influence the way in which professional practice is conducted with at-risk children and their families. Just as the personal self has the potential to impose value-laden judgements upon practice, so too the professional self, inscribed by institutional authority and power, has the potential to frame assumptions and biases (McKee, 2003).

Because child protection practice is infused with strong emotions, values and beliefs around what constitutes abuse and how society should respond, the degree to which cultural reflexivity influences professional judgement and conduct within the practice setting is important. The need for vigilance regarding the impact of theoretical cultures and the 'censorship exercised by disciplinary and institutional attachments' (Wacquant, 1998, p.226), therefore, gains significance, together with the need to recognise, work with and critique cultural reflexivity within both the realms of the personal self and the professional self.

Failure to appreciate the power of personal and professional reflexivity can create the potential for theory and practice to be built upon reflexive responses that are less to do with the client and more to do with the worker in the context of the organisation. Writing from a sociological perspective, Bourdieu (cited in Bourdieu and Wacquant, 1992, pp.68–9) cautions against such theorising:

> In my view, one of the chief sources of error in the social sciences resides in an uncontrolled relation to the object which results in the projection of this relation onto the object. What distresses me when I read some works by sociologists is that people whose profession it is to objectivize the social world prove so rarely able to objectivize themselves, and fail so often to realize that what their apparently scientific discourse talks about is not the object but their relation to the object.

In general, the literature discussing professional attitudes and how they impact on the delivery of services has been macro-focused, reinforcing the significance of aetiological explanations and their impact on the nature and extent of services provided. By contrast, theoretical cultures in the micro sense, along with personal cultural thinking, have received scant attention in the literature. It would seem important, therefore, to develop strategies that may help the worker not only to better appreciate the significance of cultural thinking, but also to understand how it might be identified and worked with as a conscious process.

Three phases in a reflective process are now offered in the following conceptual model of self-analysis (Figure 2.1). Within this model, the cultural-reflective model, the worker can identify culturally driven reactions, critically reflect upon them and explore the potential for developing reflective practice outcomes. Thus the model reinforces the possibility of reflexivity being a conscious process and, therefore, something that can be confronted and worked with as a micro-practice issue.

The phases in Figure 2.1 include processes of cultural thinking, critical reflection and reflective practice outcomes. These will now be explored in detail.

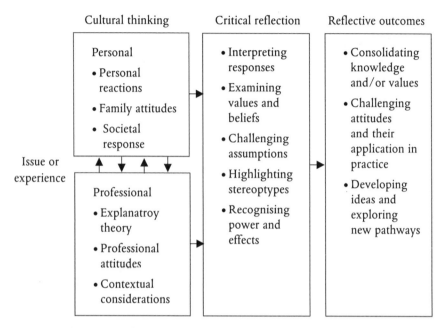

Figure 2.1: Phases in the cultural-reflective model

Cultural thinking responses

As noted earlier, tacit cultural knowledge can have the potential to influence behaviour as automatic and often unconscious responses to interactions within the environment. Whenever we confront a situation, our reactions influence our response to that situation and the situation changes as a result. The model identifies two spheres within which cultural thinking is relevant and may impact on the way in which the situation changes: the personal sphere and the professional sphere. Within the personal sphere the family provides a powerful socialising effect with respect to the developing individual. The way we view a situation or phenomena can be critically shaped by values and beliefs developed during our formative years. While family values and attitudes are inevitably filtered by other experiences within the environment, they can also be reinforced by societal values and beliefs, creating an even more compelling influence. Given the value-driven nature of abuse work, the degree to which cultural thinking influences professional judgement and conduct is important.

The professional sphere also provides a rich repository for cultural thinking. The professional self, infused with explanatory theories and professional attitudes that are contextual, can also create culturally based responses to client/worker situations. For example, if a worker has integrated knowledge about abuse aetiology that reinforces a single common explanation, then this knowledge may unwittingly restrict their exploratory investigation. Practice questions designed to confirm the theory may dominate the work at the expense of more helpful inquiry into how this particular family experiences their world. Because of this, the need to recognise, work with and critique cultural thinking in the spheres of the personal and professional self becomes important. This encourages 'critical dissection of the concepts, methods, and problematics (the worker) inherits as well as for vigilance toward the censorship exercised by disciplinary and institutional attachments' (Wacquant, 1998, p.226).

Cultural thinking responses are often automatic and outside our control; it is impossible for us not to have them. Indeed, our cultural responses – whether they relate to how we approach the work, its pace or the directions we take – become the cultural components of our practice. These, and other cultural components within a practice repertoire, if left on their own, are likely to remain constant regardless of cross-cultural differences in practice. Unchallenged, they have the potential to interfere with the practice process. However, critically reflecting on these cultural components, which emerge from an analysis of the personal and professional self, offers an opportunity to achieve more reflective practice outcomes by identifying and responding to cross-cultural misunderstandings when they occur.

Critical reflection

Reflection as a strategy within practice has been part of practice discourse for a number of years (Gould and Taylor, 1996; Schon, 1983, 1987). More recently the notion of critical reflection has taken hold (Pease and Fook, 1999). Fook (1999) draws a distinction between reflection and critical reflection in practice. Rather than merely reflecting upon or thinking about practice, a critical reflective response can be seen significantly to challenge the values and attitudes associated with professional conduct and provide a more productive means by which practice can be critiqued. Returning to the three-phase framework outlined in Figure 2.1, undertaking a critical reflective process follows the cultural thinking response phase.

Within the critical reflection phase, a process of *interpretation* is explored. Interpreting responses initially requires an identification of cultural thinking reactions. Where did the reactions come from? Can they be traced back to the domain of the personal or professional self? Carefully listening to language used within the practice relationship can help to identify these reactions (Connolly, 2003). Transcribing interviews into text can be helpful in tracking reactions, and similar processes can be used in practice (Rossiter, 1995). Carefully analysing interviews provides a rich source of material that can reveal much in terms of a worker's ability to follow cues, develop exploratory pathways and identify what interactive processes influence direction. While it is clearly unrealistic to critically reflect upon every practice encounter, doing so from time to time, with different practice relationships, can have the effect of sensitising a worker to cultural thinking responses. Here we are talking about critical reflection in retrospect, and generally it is discussed in this way (Fook, 1999). However, workers could also practice critical reflection *during* practice encounters. Being able to think about and respond to reflexive reactions during a session (and, thereby, understanding the driving forces within the interview) would seem to be preferable to fixing it up later. However, the 'fixing up' is a strong reinforcer of vigilance as the worker becomes increasingly aware of, and attuned to, cultural dominance within a practice encounter.

In addition to identifying reflexive reactions, a reflective process can encourage an examination of the *values and beliefs* underpinning these reactions. Since reactions are often buried in tacit cultural knowledge, it is likely that they will also be connected to a set of cultural values and beliefs that are reinforced within the personal and professional process of socialisation. Examining the origins and the implications of these values and beliefs is an important aspect of a critical reflective process. For example, in terms of the personal self, how does the belief system of the worker resonate with that of the family? How does the worker's experience give rise to beliefs around how this child should be protected? In terms of the professional self, how does the worker's agency influence professional cultural thinking and the subsequent service delivery to this particular family? How is practice influenced by characteristics of the *rescue* model of child welfare (Marsh and Crow, 1998)?

Concomitant with this, two associated processes are identified: the *challenging of assumptions* and the *highlighting of stereotypes*. Any critical examination of beliefs and values will also include an interrogation of the underpinning assumptions that are supportive of them. Are cultural thinking processes giving rise to cultural assumptions that unintentionally condone abusive behaviour? Is abuse being seen as a 'cultural norm' causing the worker to accommodate to abusive practices? According to Cohen (2003, p.2), issues of race can have a powerful impact on the choices that workers make:

> Sometimes race and culture may lead to more intrusive interventions, but at other times, they seem to normalize unacceptable behaviour. The cultural and racial background of families influence the specific factors that workers consider in assessing the severity of risk and level of intervention. Decisions are more likely to be made on the basis of deficits in available resources, accepted agency practice, personal values and biases, and notions of an ideal family than by application of consistent case rules.

While this notion of cultural accommodation is often discussed in the context of race and ethnicity, a range of cultural thinking environments can increase practice complexity in child care and protection. Consider, for example, child protection in the context of disability. Cultural thinking around disability is dominated by assumptions and stereotypical representations. Not surprisingly, parents of a disabled child are responded to sympathetically, and there are times when the behaviour of a disabled child can be seen to challenge the most caring parent. Given the management of difficult behaviour is frequently seen in the context of a need for constraint, is there potential for worker perception to normalise unacceptable behaviour and accommodate levels of force that they would not normally consider appropriate? And, more broadly still, do beliefs and stereotypes surrounding disability influence the ways in which services respond to disabled children's needs, interests and human rights?

Professional expertise can also be powerful in the development of theoretically reinforced assumptions and cultures. While professional expertise can, of course, enhance understanding, more importantly it can have the potential to inhibit exploratory enquiry. This is perhaps most clearly demonstrated in the adoption of a 'rescue culture' in child care and protection practice that we mentioned above. Underpinned by societal expectations that social workers will rescue children from harm – and should be punished if they don't – it is hardly surprising that more defensive cultures of practice emerge. Such cultures frequently reflect an overuse of statutory power and more conservative and intrusive interventions that will withstand public criticism if things go wrong. Nevertheless, the more forensic, interventionist approaches can have significant limitations when seen in the context of a child's need for stability and permanency. Within a risk-averse practice environment, the need to interrogate the cultural thinking underpinning the work becomes, therefore, increasingly important.

Recognising *power and its effects* is also important to understanding in a critically reflective process. Exploring power and how it operates within the clinical setting is promoted here as an important feature of critically reflective practice. It requires an understanding of the potential use of personal and professional power (Connolly, 1999) and how this may influence the direction of the work. Power, or influence, changes a course of interaction, whether exerted by the worker or the client. Using one's power to influence a process, or the behaviour of another, may be viewed negatively and can have negative effects. If a power response is an unconscious reaction to a culturally driven thinking process, the worker may not be aware of its genesis and may respond unhelpfully to a family. Notwithstanding this, power is inevitably used by both workers and families as part of the usual process of interaction and, if understood, can have the effect of positively influencing processes. Recognising power and understanding how it operates within systems of interaction is, therefore, an important component of reflective practice.

Using a critically reflective process when working through the complex area of cultural thinking has a number of benefits. Reflecting on cultural thinking can challenge unhelpful attitudes and practices that have the potential to create cultural misunderstandings. In addition, professional assessments of families can be powerfully enduring, and research has suggested that professionals are often slow to revise their judgements, even in the context of positive family change (Munro, 1999). Using a critically reflective process can, therefore, help to dislodge beliefs underpinning assessments when they are no longer relevant to the changed practice environment. While critical reflection has the potential to challenge professional practice and the need for practice change, importantly it can also confirm professional interpretations, consolidate professional knowledge, build practice wisdom and provide a sense of 'being on track'.

In general, practice literature within the child protection area has been largely contextual and dominated by research into abuse causation and behaviour. While this is clearly important, contributing as it does to a more in-depth understanding of the abuse dynamic, there has been little theorising and research into practice *process* in the abuse field. The developing nature of practice, and how cultural components impact on the work, has received less attention in the practice literature. Because the conflicting values are very much a part of the work with children and families in child care and protection, the need to explore social work praxeology – the nature of professional conduct within the practice area – becomes increasingly important. Understanding the nature of the evolving practice process, identifying the ways in which this is influenced by the personal and professional self, and reflecting upon the cultural components of practice to explore creative outcomes become necessary parts of practice evaluation and development.

In this chapter we have examined the nature of personal and professional cultural thinking and how this impacts on the work. Practice, of course, exists within yet another cultural system – the child care and protection system itself. In the same way that personal and professional cultures have the potential to impose ideas on practice, so, too, the system imposes its own set of beliefs and values that ultimately shape service delivery. This is now explored in Chapter 3, together with some suggestions about the way in which culturally responsive practice can develop within our systems of child welfare.

Chapter 3

Ethnic culture, child protection and the professional environment

The constraints and demands that characterise contemporary child protection environments invariably impact on the potential for, and the quality of, culturally responsive practices with children and their families. In general, policy informing child care and protection promotes the philosophy of best practice. This notwithstanding, efforts continue to be confounded by high numbers of child abuse notifications, funding and resource restraints and high turnover of staff. The resulting strained environment does little to enhance best practice in the field. This chapter examines the effect of such an environment on culturally responsive practice and explores the tools that assist a worker to respond appropriately to diverse situations, whatever they may be.

The changing environment of child protection

The child protection system can be defined as the organisations, most often statutory, responsible for the implementation of legislation and policies whose prime objective is to promote the welfare of children not in receipt of adequate care or control. As noted in Chapter 2, countries develop their own ways of responding to child abuse and neglect, each individual nation's child protection system developing in relation to its own socio-cultural, political and economic environment. In addition, the way in which child protection systems have developed is also influenced by factors such as the increased awareness of child abuse, and trends in fiscal retrenchment with respect to public expenditure.

Over the past 50 years, knowledge and awareness of child abuse and neglect have increased exponentially. Of course, child abuse has always been present in history but, as Dalley (2004, p.175) suggests, interest in the issue has been sporadic and thus child abuse 'has been a social issue for particular moments in time – discovered, ignored, and discovered again'. Awareness of child abuse for many countries was rekindled with the discovery of the 'battered child syndrome' (Freeman, 2000) and through the work of children's rights groups and feminist movements. In recent years, many countries have made changes to child protection policy and practice as a consequence of a major child abuse inquiry. In Britain, the Cleveland Inquiry created calls for change (Parton, Thorpe and Wattam, 1997), and the Kilkenny Incest Investigation produced similar concerns in Ireland (Buckley, 1999). These and other investigations, conducted in an environment of high-pitched media reporting and public interest, have served to place child protection systems under considerable public scrutiny. As a consequence, pressure on the child protection system to perform has escalated.

Alongside increased media attention, there have also been changes in the nature of welfare provision in many countries. Economic crises have led to fluctuations and transformations in welfare spending changing the shape and management of statutory systems. In Britain, increases in public expenditure, caused by a growth in unemployment in the 1960s, were soon followed by a global recession and a corresponding decrease in expenditure. In the US there has been a strong emphasis on reducing state welfare and a move towards 'devolution and privatization' (Morgen, 2001, p.748), while in New Zealand, economic reforms have dramatically impacted upon the way in which services have developed in that country. In many cases around the world, efforts have been made to control public expenditure in child protection organisations by employing private sector managers in order to sharpen the management of social services. Davis and Garrett (2004, p.22) describe this as 'the promotion of managerialism in social work organisations'. This has produced a change in the culture of service development with professionals largely being isolated from processes of decision-making (Belgrave, 2004, p.38).

These economic and managerial changes in culture have fundamentally changed child protection practice. Garrett (2003, p.2) describes the transformation as the 'remaking of social work with children and families'. Child protection systems internationally, constrained by limited resources and subjected to intense public scrutiny, have turned their focus toward developing procedures of accountability with the aim of reducing the margin for error. Increasingly, they have looked to the introduction of tools and instruments to improve practice.

Instruments and tools in child protection

Particularly popular in Western child protection systems in recent times has been the introduction of risk assessment frameworks. Parton *et al.* (1997, p.16) argue that risk 'has become the key signifier for child abuse, both in policy developments and for practical decision-making'. Risk frameworks assume that child abuse is 'identifiable, predictable and preventable via the development and application of scientific research' (p.45). These frameworks for identifying risk are used at various points within the child protection process.

The focus on instruments and tools represents the assumption that rigorous and robust child protection practice is more likely with the use of tested, researched techniques. In other words, competent and professional practice becomes 'an exercise in technical rationality' (Parton, 2003, p.2). There are, however, limitations in understanding practice in this way. Child protection practice is far from an exact science. Indeed, it is an incredibly complex enterprise, at times so convoluted that it can be difficult to see how a technical approach may be of value. As Parton (2003, p.2) explains:

> 'Knowing' in such situations is invariably *tacit* and *implicit*. It develops from dialogue with people about the situation, through which the practitioner can come to understand the uniqueness, uncertainty and potential value conflicts that must be addressed and thereby reaches 'a new theory of the unique case' that informs actions.

Nevertheless, the drive toward a more scientific culture with the introduction of instruments and tools to support worker decision-making is commendable and risk assessment frameworks are just one example of the instruments and tools which have found favour in recent years. Nevertheless, given the increasing ethnic diversity of societies, consideration must be given to how the instruments and tools enhance the ability of the child protection practitioner to be culturally responsive in the work that they do. In this administratively focused environment, culturally responsive practice appears to gain little traction. All too often the dominating factors have more to do with bureaucratic issues, while the detail and skills of practice become of secondary concern (Charles and Wilton, 2004; Parton and O'Byrne, 2000). Furthermore, according to Charles and Wilton (2004, p.182):

completion of administrative tasks, initially seen as bureaucratic burdens, creates an illusion to the worker, his/her manager and the organisation of social work well done, of partnership and agreement, and of risks assessed and managed, yet their fulfilment may have nothing to do with the real needs of service users.

Instruments, tools and culture

Despite the concentration in recent years on administrative functions within child protection organisations, there have been attempts to incorporate cultural information into instruments and tools. In this regard, the main focus has been to assist the development of child protection practitioners' understanding and knowledge about the culture of specific ethnic groups. Development of the practitioner is achieved through their attendance at courses and workshops, and, sometimes, by the addition of ethnic-specific cultural guidelines which sit alongside the particular instrument or tool the practitioner employs. While these initiatives might be seen as a move forward in terms of supporting culturally responsive practice, they also present a number of challenges.

First, there is the tension between attempting to provide a competent child protection service within the stressful, under-resourced public systems. High workloads and high staff turnover within the child protection environment are likely to lead to situations where child protection practitioners are inadequately trained to manage complex child protection work. This requires that workers be trained in the use of instruments and tools necessary for the job, as well as needing to be prepared for cross-cultural encounters – and all this has to be done with haste. Usually this is handled by creating short-term, one-off training courses or workshops. To illustrate this: the relatively new child protection practitioner attends a three-day workshop, the focus of which is the organisation's risk assessment process. At best, half a day may be devoted to aspects of culture. Cultural context and history are crammed into these precious hours, along with the transmission of core cultural values and snippets of engagement techniques that will help the new practitioner to avoid cultural transgression. Our new child protection worker leaves the workshop either assuming they have all the information needed to work cross-culturally, or in fear of being culturally incompetent but unlikely to get any further support. There are parallels here with Margaret Mead's exploits into Samoa in the 1920s. Convinced that Samoan culture was simple and uncomplicated, she wrote in her introduction to *Coming of age in Samoa* that a trained student could 'master the fundamental structure of a primitive society in a few months' (Freeman, 1983, p.285). Given she only had a few months in the community, and with limited skills in Samoan language, it is hardly surprising that she so seriously misinterpreted her findings in what is now considered a deeply flawed account of Samoan culture. There are dangers in making assumptions about cross-cultural issues and processes. Quick-fix training solutions can sometimes make things worse rather than better.

Returning to training then: workshops that focus on the specific history and core values of a particular ethnic culture, while helpful to a degree, may also contribute to assumptions of homogeneity across cultures. How will the worker respond if the client does not hold the values that the worker expected of someone from that specific culture? If the client behaves differently, what kind of response would it trigger in the worker? Would the worker assume that the client had become alienated from their culture? It is clear that, if used independently, approaches focusing on specific cultural group content are simplistic and insufficient for the development of culturally responsive practice. Indeed, according to McPhatter (1997, p.256), 'these efforts...have not addressed culturally effective practice in a comprehensive and sustained manner, and have been inadequate'.

Finally, tools or instruments are used in child protection organisations in the belief that they are culturally neutral, universal and appropriate to all. This assumption fails to recognise that any approach to child protection practice is closely related to the context and cultural environment within which it is developed. Given that tools are generally developed from research undertaken with Western, English-speaking people, they may not be applicable to other ethnic groups.

It is clear that developing culturally responsive practices in child care and protection presents many challenges. An alternative to the administrative approach can be found in postmodernist perspectives.

Social constructivism

The term *social constructivism* has been developed by Lee and Greene (1999, p.25) to describe a different way of 'thinking about and doing clinical practice, teaching clinical social work courses, and conducting workshops and training'. Social constructivism is the result of an amalgamation of two metatheories, constructivism and social constructionism, which have tended to be used interchangeably in the literature (Franklin, 1995; Lee and Greene,

1999) – which is not surprising given the similarities which exist between the two. Both theories consider that people have agency within their lives, and both see the environment and the person as being intricately connected. As a point of difference, constructivists call attention to cognitive structures and the processes of human development, while social constructionists emphasise the importance of language, and socio-historical and cultural processes in understanding one's view of the social world. Each metatheory can be thought of as influencing a range of practice approaches. For example, constructivism has influenced the development of psychoanalytic and cognitive approaches, while social constructionism can be linked with strengths and narrative approaches (Franklin, 1995).

Lee and Greene's (1999) amalgamation of these metatheories represents an acknowledgement of the similarities between the two approaches. Their resulting social constructivist framework encourages the practitioner to become familiar with the uniqueness of an individual's ethnic identity and social context. The framework also acknowledges that these situated meanings influence an individual's perception of the issue at hand and their resulting help-seeking behaviour. The framework can be applied to child protection practice situations as a guide to assessment, and even though it does not specifically cover ethnic-specific group information it can be greatly enhanced by incorporating it. Additionally, it is important that the framework be examined alongside practitioner attitude, knowledge and skills information that we discussed in Chapter 1.

A social constructivist framework for child protection practice

Before exploring the framework, it is important that we consider the notion of 'expert' within practice. Traditional social work approaches tend to position the practitioner as the expert knower who, as a consequence of their skills and experience, can develop insight into the world of the client – indeed, may be seen to 'know' the client better than the client may know themselves. Alternative approaches, consistent with the constructivist framework, emphasise the importance of the practitioner as learner and the client as guide or expert to their own cultural identity. As Leigh (1998, p.79) suggests:

> The social worker should remember that the objective of the ethnographic approach is to learn about cultural behaviour, values, language, and worldviews of the person who is representative of the cultural group, and to use this information in a process that results in treatment planning and

intervention strategies that are congruent with the cultural demands of the person.

Therefore, the child protection practitioner may ask, 'What information does my client know that I can discover?' as opposed to 'What expert knowledge do I possess?'. This stance does not negate knowledge of child abuse or of the dynamics of oppression, prejudice and discrimination that the child protection practitioner needs to possess. Indeed, this knowledge is critical if workers are to foster safe practices when working with family violence and child abuse. Rather, it recognises that these are so strongly interrelated with cultural values and beliefs that it is necessary to be able to understand how *this* person understands their world and how *these* beliefs, attitudes and behaviours interact with the dynamics of abuse.

The role of the child protection practitioner is generally to substantiate whether abuse or neglect has occurred, to ensure the safety of the child, and to provide or arrange ameliorative services. Culture has featured, at times not in a useful way, in each of these practice areas. Statements by social workers, such as 'Harsh physical discipline is a part of their culture', or 'It's [child abuse] a key part of their culture', illustrate how culture at times has been used as an explanatory argument suggesting that child abuse or neglect has occurred because of the family's identification with a particular ethnic group. These same perspectives inform child practitioners' conceptualisation of the barriers to working in a culturally responsive way. Hence, a family's ethnic identification can be framed as a barrier to successful outcomes. A social constructivist framework supports the practitioner to move away from essentialist notions to successfully negotiate meaning and make sense of the uniqueness of the client's circumstance and experience. Here, rather than being a barrier, culture becomes an enhancer of successful outcomes.

Before moving on to discuss the social constructivist framework in detail, it is important to note that this framework is suggested here as a way of promoting understanding about the self as a mediator between experience and response. It is a tool that can be most usefully used at the beginning of contact with a family and revisited many times throughout the process of child protection work. The framework may also be used alongside other tools and instruments. As stated earlier, cultural identity is informed by multiple aspects and culture is not a concept that belongs only to migratory populations or minority ethnic groups. Social constructivism can be applied whenever workers confront diversity in practice – essentially in all practice encounters. As King Keenan (2004, p.540) notes: 'Social workers will listen, explore, conceptualize, and intervene in a more complex and effective manner if every client– worker relationship is perceived as constituted by a combination of similarities and differences…'.

Furthermore, it is the internalised culture of the client or family that the child protection practitioner is required to understand. The focus is on understanding the client or family in context, aspects of which may be presented by the client or family as risks or strengths. It is the client or family's experience and interpretation of these aspects that is of greatest importance.

The social constructivist framework in essence supports the notion that the self is a mediator between culture and behaviour, as illustrated in Figure 3.1. In the social constructivist framework, the self is contextualised and represents the link between influencing cultural variables and feeling, thinking and behavioural responses. Hence, Lee and Greene (1999, p.29) argue:

> culture and related social processes influence the development of individuals' self-definition and, consequently, their thinking, feeling, and behaviour… [P]eople from different social groups construct their own cultural self-definitions in a way consistent with and viable in their own cultural context.

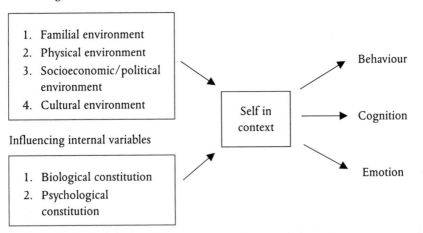

Influencing external variables

1. Familial environment
2. Physical environment
3. Socioeconomic/political environment
4. Cultural environment

Influencing internal variables

1. Biological constitution
2. Psychological constitution

Self in context

Behaviour

Cognition

Emotion

Figure 3.1: The self as mediator between culture and behaviour. Source: A social constructivist framework for integrating cross-cultural issues in teaching clinical social work (Lee and Greene, 1999). Reproduced with permission.

External variables

Both external and internal cultural variables influence the self in context. External variables are those influences which exist in a person's environmental context. The familial environment is an important external variable that helps the worker to understand how family is defined. For example, does the definition of family include parents, partners, siblings, children, grandparents, uncles and aunts, those who are biologically related and/or those who are not? Other aspects may include identifying who is in the family, the role each person plays, the status of individual family members, the connections between them. These connections may be physical in the sense of geographical location, or they may be emotional in terms of the depth and strength of the attachment. Family values and beliefs and the family's relationships with others are further aspects of the familial environment.

The external variable, the family's physical environment, highlights the need for the worker to gain an understanding of how the family perceives their physical environment, their home and their surrounding network, including the resources and amenities available to them. Often associated with the physical environment, the socioeconomic-political environment includes the economic influences impacting on the family and their capacity to function. Examining this environment may involve the worker in considering factors such as financial status and the influence of this on family dynamics.

Another variable is the cultural environment, which relates to the client or family's ethnic identification and the values, beliefs and experiences which arise from this. It may include experiences involving spirituality, migration and community belonging or isolation, in addition to experiences of oppression, prejudice and discrimination. In relation to child protection practice, the client or family's experience and views of parenting and childhood, based on the values, beliefs and practices of a particular cultural environment, are central.

Internal variables

Internal variables within the social constructivist framework also influence the self. Although it may appear confusing or paradoxical to have biological and psychological aspects identified within a constructivist framework, here they refer to physical and psychological well-being. It is imperative that the child protection practitioner understands the client or family's conceptualisations of illness, health and disability. Examples of contextual information may include the client or family's interpretation of individual illness, the meaning of the symptoms and the perceived causes. Understanding the cultural thinking surrounding the interpretation of illness will help the worker to understand, for example, ritualistic processes and how to assist in bringing about change in abusive practices.

Problem perception and solution

Undeniably, child protection investigations and assessment processes exist to reduce the risk of child maltreatment and address its effects (DePanfilis, 2000). The social constructivist framework promotes the notion that thoughts, feelings and actions are influenced by external and internal variables that are cultural in origin and, as a consequence, that each individual who enters the child protection system is unique. A logical consequence to this is that perceptions of the child protection problem will be unique to each client or family, as will help-seeking behaviour (Lee and Greene, 1999). Understanding how the client or family perceives the problem enables child protection practitioners to work in a more culturally responsive way with clients or families in developing viable solutions (Lee and Greene, 1999). This process is illustrated in Figure 3.2.

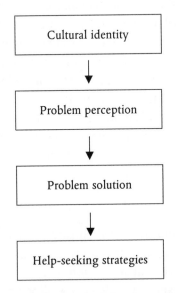

Figure 3.2: Cultural identity shaping both perceptions and solutions. Source: adapted from A social constructivist framework for integrating cross-cultural issues in teaching clinical social work *(Lee and Greene, 1999). Reproduced with permission.*

As Cooper (2001) suggests, agreement on aspects of child abuse and neglect which are concrete in nature must follow through to an understanding of other meanings that underlie what is apparent. Cooper (p.732) describes the situation where there is little room for argument if one can see that a child has a bruise on his face:

> however, the meanings in context of a child's injury are not 'revealed' through objective facts or through 'expert' objective assessment or diagnosis. An agreed meaning, understanding and potential for change can only be co-constructed, with the service user and their social relationships and networks, within a situated organisational and multi-agency context.

The following example highlights the importance of the connection between client in context, problem perception and problem solution:

Sam and Kelly are parents who are involved with protective services following a notification from the children's school. The school advised that the children presented as unkempt, often without lunch or shoes, and would fall asleep in class every afternoon. Sam and Kelly both have limited formal education; both speak English as a second language. They live in a two-bedroom home in a lower-socioeconomic part of town. They are strongly involved with their local church community. Sam works long shift work hours in a clothing factory, while Kelly is responsible for the house and children. The children are aged 12, 10 and 7 years, and it is not the first time concern has been expressed regarding their well-being. Four years previously, child protection services in another city were involved; the family had then moved on and contact was lost.

On further investigation, it is discovered that Sam had been married to Kelly's sister, Jane, who had passed away 13 years ago. Before her death, Jane had discovered that Sam and Kelly were having an affair. It transpires that Jane, on her deathbed, had placed a curse on Sam and Kelly. In the ensuing 13 years, Kelly and Sam both believed in the curse and that it was the reason for their continued bad luck. Kelly, in particular, is convinced the curse is real. She appears agitated and troubled in her discussions with the practitioners. Previous interventions following similar child protection notifications included sending Kelly and Sam on parenting skills courses, and both parents had been encouraged to attend counselling. Even though Kelly and Sam had shared their views of the curse and its impact on their lives, they each felt that previous workers had thought they were crazy. Prior to gaining formal professional assistance Kelly and Sam sought help from a few key family members who have offered emotional support over the years, although there were some sections of the family who would not have contact with Kelly and Sam because of the perceived dangers of the curse. Additionally, the church Kelly and Sam attended has been supportive and willing to help.

This time, once the child protection practitioners understand the parents' perception of the problem, they ask Kelly and Sam what would be considered a viable solution. The parents agree that a traditional cultural process of removing the curse would be best. This is a process the family have wanted to follow for some time but they lack the financial resources to do so since the solution requires the family travelling to another, faraway city. With the support of the protective services and the local church community, traditional practices are employed to remove the curse. The school, a few months later, reports they have no further concerns about the children's well-being. The parents appear calm and relaxed and able to move on with their lives.

Highlighting the connection between problem perception and solution, this example draws attention to the differing responses from protective services. Not all workers will be at ease with culturally driven responses, and the comfort and personal belief system of workers are likely to influence practice responses. In this example, initially, the centrality of the clients' spiritual beliefs did not feature in the professional analysis of the problem, even though this is how the clients interpreted the difficulties being experienced. Hence, the solutions initially pursued were not responsive to the ethnic culture of the family.

Culture is a resource that can be harnessed and used to build solutions in child care and protection practice. Aligning solutions with the cultural identity of the family then provides the potential for family-centred responses. Swidler (1986) describes culture as a 'tool-kit' and this metaphor for culture has been enhanced by Forte (1999). The primary notion is that people are solution-finders, and, therefore, within each cultural group there exists a range of tools available to solve problems. These are otherwise known as strategies of action. In applying the tool-kit metaphor, it becomes important to suspend the prevailing notion that one approach is the right approach for all. For any problem identified there is a range of responses, highlighting the 'image of the person as an active and creative user of culture' (Forte, 1999, p.55). Solutions need to align with the client or family's preferred strategies of action. Problem solutions must also take into consideration help-seeking preferences.

Help-seeking approaches

Lee and Greene (1999, p.34) describe help-seeking approaches as incorporating 'sources of help, the nature of help, the method adopted in solving the problem and the outcome of the healing'. Given that protective services are most frequently involved with families who do not want to be involved voluntarily, the term 'help-seeking' may seem an unlikely fit. However, the help-seeking literature (Dale, 2004; Kaukinen, 2002; Lee and Greene, 1999; Schonert-Reichl and Muller, 1996; Zink, Elder and Jacobsen, 2003) is careful to point out that help-seeking can be described as a continuum, where an individual may seek out help informally with friends and family for some time before seeking help from professionals. It is possible that individuals reluctantly involved with child protection services have, at earlier points, attempted to deal with the troubles that beset them.

The importance of understanding help-seeking strategies can be found in examples from the family violence literature. Kaukinen (2002) makes the point that often victims of partner violence are perceived as passive in their victimisation. Kaukinen's research into the help-seeking strategies of women victims of intimate partner violence demonstrates the agency of victims. Rather than passive actors, women employed a range of coping and survival strategies. Kaukinen identifies three distinct help-seeking strategies: first, substantial strategies which involve seeking help from informal sources (e.g. family and friends) and formal sources (e.g. social services, doctors or the police); second, family/friend strategies which involve seeking help from informal sources; and third, minimal strategies where women are unlikely to actively seek help from any source.

Zink *et al.* (2003) explore the role children play in their mothers' management of intimate partner violence. Their findings suggest that mothers consider a wide array of factors when coping with the violence, including their 'attachment to the perpetrator, the support or lack of support from family and friends, and the help received or not received from professionals and community agencies' (p.590). One of the biggest fears experienced by the women was that they would lose their children if child protection agencies learned of the intimate partner violence. This fear is confirmed by Keller and McDade (2000, p.305), whose survey of low-income parents' attitudes to parenting help concluded that parents perceived the actions of child protection organisations as 'arbitrary, unfair and punitive to parents'.

In the example of Kelly and Sam above, help-seeking strategies were initially located primarily within their own ethnic cultural community. Early professional responses neglected the cultural interpretations of the problem, and were then unable to harness the potential of culturally driven solutions. Of course, not all cultural solutions or, indeed, family interpretations of a child abuse issue will be acceptable. A social constructivist approach does not advocate that the practitioner agree with the client or family's perception of the problem if it represents risk to the child or to others. However, understanding world-views, whatever they are, provides the practitioner with a realistic place from which to begin work with people and with a clear idea of the difficulties and strengths that may emerge as they work to reduce harm and build supports.

There are many pressures which characterise child protection systems, including fewer resources, high workloads and high turnover of staff. By its very nature, child protection practice is never going to be a simple and smooth-sailing enterprise. While the framework advocated in this chapter does not necessarily require greater monetary or time resources, it does require recognition of the fundamental importance of culture in child protection work. Because ethnic identity and cultural difference are components of human identity and not confined to the domain of those who are 'different' to mainstream society, they impact on our interactions every day. This being the case, culturally responsive practice becomes mainstream practice as we work across the inevitable domains of difference. The challenge for child care and protection workers is to recognise the potential of culture as a tool through which creative solutions can be found.

Part Two

Working with cultures in child protection

Chapter 4

Childhood cultures, care and protection

In this book we have reinforced the notion that human perceptions and assessments of the social world are likely to say more about the perceiver than the persons under study. This is starkly illuminated when we look at adult perceptions of children. One only has to take a wander along the corridors of national art galleries to see the ways in which children have been seen by adults over time. Fully dressed in miniature adult clothes, children have been depicted as small adults just waiting to get bigger (Lavalette and Cunningham, 2002). Take for example, Ngatau Omahuru, shown in Figure 4.1 wearing an Eton suit and bow tie. He can only be five or six years of age, yet how unchildlike he appears. His expression, angry, while at the same time sad and lost, provides a poignant illustration of cultures colliding – adult/child, Western/non-Western. In a story befitting a Hollywood film, he was abducted from his Maori family in the late 1860s and adopted by New Zealand's Prime Minister, Sir William Fox, shortly thereafter finding his way to the drawing rooms of London (Walker, 2001). To the surprise and displeasure of some, particularly his adoptive parents, although he was raised as New Zealand's first Maori gentleman lawyer, he went back to his people when he reached the age of 19. He never returned to the law, preferring to end his days teaching Maori language by home study.

Through contemporary eyes such photographs may look amusingly cute. We may think that modern childhood little reflects the harsh realities of child-hood a century ago. Indeed, modern writers have raised questions about the motives behind early representations of childhood, suggesting that they are

Figure 4.1: Portrait of Ngatau Omahuru, Reproduced with kind permission from the Alexander Turnball Library, Wellington, New Zealand, PA2-2494.

less to do with the society seeing children as miniature adults and more to do with parents illustrating the beauty and social status of their offspring with a view to securing good marriages (Lavalette and Cunningham, 2002). Yet many of these early ideas – that adults know more about children and what is best for them – have continued to dominate adult cultural thinking and serve to remain a powerful shaper, not only of the way we think about children but also of how we respond to them.

Although child protection work is by its nature child-oriented, decisions are invariably made by adults and are based on what adults consider to be in the child's best interests. Practice tends to operate from an adult point of view, with little reference to childhood cultures and the need for children to be involved in the processes that concern them. In this chapter we explore child-hood cultures, and the ways in which the agency of children has been promoted in the practice of child care and protection. We look at the 'new social studies of childhood' perspective and review research that has been undertaken with children and young people who have experienced statutory systems of care. We suggest that listening to their voices directly, as opposed to relying on how parents or workers interpret their experience, may help us to understand better the world of childhood and find ways to create more child-responsive approaches to practice.

Understanding children

Because we have all been children we tend to have pretty strong and clear ideas about what it is to be a child. When we recall our childhood experiences they inevitably reflect our unique experience of time and place. Yet how often do our practice views reflect assumptions that are based on how we ourselves experienced childhood? How are our views about children's attitudes toward their parents shaped by our own? In recent years there has been a growing interest in childhood studies and the need to better understand childhood cultures from children themselves. According to Lavalette and Cunningham (2002, pp.23–4):

> children occupy and conduct themselves in worlds that are full of meaning for them, but about which adults are, at least partially, ignorant. These are largely 'children's childhoods'. Children are best placed to describe and analyse this world, better at any rate than adult outsiders.

The 'new social studies of childhood' have been influential in developing the notion of the child as 'being' (Holloway and Valentine, 2000) to be understood according to the child's own view of the world. In fact, the 'new social studies of childhood' are not exactly 'new' and are now over 20 years old. Nevertheless the approach is 'new' in the sense that it breaks away from traditional ideas about childhood. Since the 1980s sociological writers have been developing their thinking about childhood cultures and how they impact on children and the child's sense of agency. Rejecting traditional developmental frameworks that focus on relatively fixed and universal stages of development, sociological theories have supported social constructivist notions of childhood that facilitate better understandings of children's agency and cultural variation (Sanders, 2004; Thomas and O'Kane, 2000). These approaches have encouraged a greater emphasis on qualitative methodologies, laying stress upon the importance of children's meaning-making rather than relying on adult-defined perceptions.

Perhaps not surprisingly, researchers seek to influence child care and protection practice by their research. The new social studies of childhood challenge us to ensure that practice is based on research that harnesses the 'voices' of children and is not only filtered through adult perceptions and definitions. A review of the research relating to children's views of their experiences of statutory care systems suggests that we seek the views of children far less often than we might. There is considerable evidence to suggest a research preference toward asking adults how they think children experience systems of care. There is also an overwhelming use of research instruments developed by adults to test children against adult-determined criteria. While it is clearly important to quantify how systems of care impact on children's well-being, it is also important to note that by comparison we rarely ask children directly how they experience it. Yet children provide crucial information about their experiences of being in care, and can also provide advice on how we interpret what they say. What they have to say is critical to our understanding of the child care and protection processes we develop to address their needs.

Research from the child's perspective

A number of methodological factors contribute to the difficulties of gaining an understanding of children's perspectives of their time in out-of-home care. For example, Gilbertson and Barber (2002) note the high levels of distress in children that prevents their participation in research studies. Furthermore, Berrick, Frasch and Fox (2000, p.119) contend, 'administrative, political, legal, and pragmatic barriers...conspire to limit researchers' access to and contact with foster children'. Yet the views of children have been sought and have added to our understanding of the impact child protection processes and systems of care have on the lives of the children themselves.

Early research generally focused on retrospective studies. More recent research has explored the experiences of children currently in care. Several themes emerge from these studies. These include the children's lack of knowledge of the circumstances leading up to their entry into care, their lack of participation and consultation in the decision-making process, their level of satisfaction with their experiences of being in care, their contact with their biological families and their relationship with their social workers.

Leaving home and entering care

Studies from the US indicate that, in trying to make sense of their experiences of being taken into care, children provide a variety of explanations: they feel they have either been 'given away' and are 'to blame for the event', have been 'taken away' and 'have no personal control over the event', or 'they chose and actually orchestrated the event' (Fox, Frasch and Berrick, 2000, p.71). In one study involving interviews with 59 children aged 11 to 14 years, a large proportion of children (40%) were confused and did not know why they had been removed from their homes, and they had little input into the decisions being made for them (58%). The methods used to remove them from their home (e.g. police and caseworkers arriving at the school or at the home) were also of concern: many were left feeling angry and embarrassed. At the same time many children were aware that the situation in their homes put them at risk while, in the case of half of the children in the study, other members of the family or friends had attempted to help the family prior to state intervention (Johnson, Yoken and Voss, 1995).

For young people in foster care in London, being taken into care was associated with sudden, unexpected and unpleasant events. The study (Baldry and Kemmis, 1998), using a questionnaire and interviews, involved 71 young people: 35 chose to participate in interviews and 36 chose to complete a questionnaire. The young people spoke of the way they coped with such an unexpected event as being taken into care:

> The sudden separation and placement without introductions at night have left a long-lasting impact on me.

> I was in the police van with my sister and it was a stuffy night and Mum had made some lemonade. Mum asked the police if I could have some; they said 'yes', but drove away when she went indoors to get it.

> [I needed] more time to get ready to move into foster placement as I didn't know what to expect. (Baldry and Kemmis, 1998, p.37)

The young people were, however, aware of the reasons for being taken into care and the experience of the placement was positive for the majority.

Consistent with other studies, Cashmore and Paxman's (1996) review of Australian studies indicates that children and young people were not given information about their families or why they were in care. One study involved interviews and focus groups with a representative group of 66 children and young people from 8 to 18 years who were living in foster care. Young people expressed a lack of understanding about what was happening:

> I remember no one ever talked about it. Since I've become independent, I've found out myself by asking my mother and Lisa [worker]. (Cashmore and Paxman, 1996, p.11)

Others were uncertain about what support they should have received, and didn't always know their rights. In Smith *et al.*'s (1999) small qualitative study (n=10) of children in foster and kinship care in New Zealand, some children clearly understood the circumstances that brought them into care; over half did not. Some were infants when they entered care. One child had very few memories of that time:

> I was crying. I didn't stop crying for ages. I can still remember me picking up a bottle and chucking it on the floor. It was the only thing I can remember. (Smith *et al.*, 1999, p.45)

Participation in decision-making

The influence of previous practices, where children were not invited to be part of the decision-making process, tends to blur the distinction between children expressing their views and asking for what they want (Cashmore and O'Brien, 2001; Munro, 2001). While legislation encourages children's participation in decision-making, messages from the research suggest that children do not feel their views are invited, accepted, or respected. Yet even being listened to helps, as this young person indicates:

> There is a person called A who lives up the road, she is a big part of my life, because she sits down and talks and I can let things out... I can let more things out with A – she listens, not many people do that. Not many people listen to what I have got to say. (Thomas and O'Kane, 2000, p.831)

In a recent study of kinship care, Doolan, Nixon and Lawrence (2004) examined the views of 37 British children who responded to their survey and 11 children who agreed to be interviewed. The children indicated the need for them to be more knowledgeable about what was happening, and more involved in the decisions made about them:

> [The social worker] came round in secret and saw my aunt and uncle. My cousin told me she had been and she had told them I had been depressed and wanted to be with Mum. I was worried I might get kicked out. She got hold of the wrong end of the stick.

> I can't do anything without the social worker knowing. To go and stay with friends they need to have six weeks' notice. I'm embarrassed about having them police checked. (Doolan *et al.*, 2004, pp.40–2)

The degree to which children are informed about the circumstances that led to their coming into care, what is happening to them and their involvement in the decision-making process vary considerably: some are consulted and have their wishes taken into account, others have no involvement (Smith *et al.*,

1999). Studies reveal that children feel the judicial system does not treat them well or explain what is happening (Wilson and Conroy, 1999); they do not feel consulted about decisions that are being made for them (Cashmore and Paxman, 1996), including where they would like to live and their contact with their original family (Smith *et al.*, 1999). However, this is not always the case for other children, who are often aware that other people make those decisions for them or that circumstances prevent them from contacting their families and siblings (Smith *et al.*, 1999).

Children, particularly those who have experienced abuse, value participation in discussions about what is to happen to them and are more likely to accept the outcomes when they are involved. Yet some children and young people are often cynical about the effectiveness of their participation when the options they are given are limited and their views are either ridiculed or not taken seriously (Cashmore and O'Brien, 2001). Furthermore, the views of some young people are not considered and their education, development or preparation for leaving care are not supported, which leaves them feeling abandoned (Harker *et al.*, 2003; Yates, 2001).

That children want opportunities to participate in their care is clearly evident. As Cashmore and O'Brien's (2001) study reveals, they want to know the content of their files, to be informed about the process and procedures and to know what choices are open to them. They also want to have someone they can trust, who will listen to them and act as an advocate if they need to make a complaint. And they want access to complaints procedures. However, the children in the study said they were concerned at the way issues of confidentiality and privacy were undermined by the numerous professionals involved in their care. This made them reluctant to 'share their thoughts and feelings' in case it was written down for others to read (p.14).

Some of the young people in the study by Baldry and Kemmis (1998) indicated that they were able to attend reviews and felt their contribution was welcomed, although some felt they were not listened to; most had read their care plans, although the majority felt that they had not been provided with information about their rights. Children also indicated that they were satisfied with the review process and felt their social workers had prepared them well. By comparison, the children in Munro's (2001, p.131) study found the review process less than satisfactory, and they felt 'powerless and frustrated' when the outcome of what was discussed at the review did not match their expectations.

Satisfaction with care

Positive aspects of foster care for children include the feeling of being loved, cared for and supported, having someone who will listen and understand them, feeling they belong, that they fit in and are 'part of the family'. Having material things, such as a room of their own and pocket money, and being taken on outings were also important to them (Baldry and Kemmis, 1998; Fox *et al.*, 2000; Sinclair, Wilson and Gibbs, 2001). Some children felt they could take their concerns to their foster caregivers and that they would receive emotional and practical support from them (Fox *et al.*, 2000; Schofield, 2001).

Children in Smith *et al.*'s (1999) study were happy about the care they were receiving, several describing their caregivers as 'nice'. The children felt that they could talk to their caregivers, and got on well with them even if they were 'sometimes a bit grouchy' (p.78). They had mixed responses in terms of their relationships with foster siblings: some got on well with them, others didn't. Some of the young people in Cashmore and Paxman's (1996) study indicated that they would have liked to have been adopted by their foster caregivers. Indeed, young people from foster placements are more likely to maintain contact with caregivers after discharge than young people in other forms of care. Several studies indicate that while children feel that being in a foster home is the best thing for them and that their quality of life has improved, they also miss their biological families and ideally want to live with them (Fox *et al.*, 2000; Sinclair *et al.*, 2001).

Young people in Sinclair *et al.*'s (2001, p.23) questionnaire study of 150 children in care expressed concern about their experiences:

> Social workers have not done anything I liked. Up to now they have moved me around a lot, specially from different schools with change of addresses. And it's hard to keep making new friends and fitting in. The social worker should not call so much at my home and stop asking me the same things over and over again, especially about my past. I want to forget all that. I would like my foster carer to adopt me. No one asks me about that!

In a large study involving interviews with 250 children in care, Wilson and Conroy (1999) explored the children's feelings of satisfaction with their placement, caregivers, care workers and their response to child welfare and its contracted providers. Children were generally positive about their living conditions and their caseworkers. Children in family foster care, however, were more likely to feel loved and safe, with few differences between those in kin and non-kinship care, than children in group care. Similar findings are reported in Australian studies by Delfabbro, Barber and Bentham (2002) where the majority of children (80%) felt secure, happy and supported, although children in foster care were more satisfied with their placement than those in residential care.

Young people in Cashmore and Paxman's study (1996, p.41) said that while they wanted 'limits' and to feel 'safe' they also wanted stable, continuous care with people who were 'understanding', 'flexible' and 'willing to listen'. Although most of the children in Johnson *et al.*'s (1995) study reported that they got on well with their foster caregivers, some felt that caregivers needed to know more about children's histories and personalities, how to help and how to take care of children, and should 'know the rules'. Once in care, few children were able to attend the same school, they were living in new neighbourhoods and having to make new friends. For some this meant an improvement: better schools and neighbourhoods, and involvement in extra-curricular activities. But over a third said they missed their friends.

Studies also indicate a high degree of satisfaction with kinship care, which is generally less disruptive than stranger foster care in terms of established social relationships and interaction. In the main, when cared for by relatives, children feel loved and safe and have good experiences (Cashmore and Paxman, 1996; Fox *et al.*, 2000; Wilson and Conroy, 1999). Some, however, have bad experiences citing unreasonable rules, derogatory comments made about their parents, lack of access to their parents, lack of privacy, physical violence, being treated like a slave, and not being trusted or able to pursue their own interests (Cashmore and Paxman, 1996).

Negative experiences of being in care are not uncommon. Studies reveal that children often have strong feelings of being different from their foster families. This can include differences in surname (some want the same name as the foster family, others prefer to retain their own name); differences in family styles, backgrounds, ethnicity (38% in one study), religion (27%), food, language (22.5% spoke a first language other than English), and personalities; as well as conflicting opinions on discipline. Some children also experience discrimination in terms of being treated differently from biological children: having to do more chores or not being included in treats, special events or outings (Cashmore and Paxman, 1996; Fox *et al.*, 2000). In several studies children cited other difficulties, such as the number of people involved in planning their future and the need to contact social services when they wanted to join in activities outside the home (Cashmore and Paxman, 1996; Sinclair *et al.*, 2001; Wilson and Conroy, 1999).

Contact with families

Studies reveal the importance of maintaining contact between children and their families of origin. In general, children want more contact with their families (Baldry and Kemmis, 1998; Fox *et al.*, 2000; Thomas and O'Kane, 1999; Yates, 2001). Some spoke of the importance of extended family, especially grandparents:

> I would like to see my nan and granddad because they have done everything for me and I love them very much. I can only see them if my mum stops lying to them about me, because my mum had turned them against me. Because they don't like my father they take it out on me, but I still see my dad. I see my dad all the time. (Baldry and Kemmis, 1998, p.37)

Siblings were also important:

> I love my brothers and sisters and I really want to see them…but I haven't seen them for the last 3 years now. (Boy aged 10) (Thomas and O'Kane, 1999, p.380)

For children who have no contact at all with their parents, contact with extended family is particularly important.

On the other hand, some children in a New Zealand study indicated that they would prefer less contact with their families. One child who was interviewed said:

> If you see [mother] tell her I'm not going to come home forever… I haven't seen her. [And I'm] glad. She'll never whip me again. (Smith *et al.*, 1999, p.101)

In the study by Thomas and O'Kane (1999, p.380) some children felt they had no option but to see their family even when they did not want to:

> The very first time I went they didn't let me visit or anything, they just took me there. This time I visited, but I didn't really want to come here. They just made me come. (Boy aged 8)

Nevertheless for some children, 'the birth mother was still a vivid and central character in their lives even when, as in [some] cases, she was mainly a source of distress' (Munro, 2001, p.132). Children in Munro's study, however, also expressed dissatisfaction at the attitudes of professionals towards their birth mothers and the way contact with their birth family was managed, and they wanted more say in the amount of contact they had. One study (Johnson *et al.*,

1995) reported that 50 per cent of children said they missed their families most of the time; they had worries about returning home and were aware that before they could return home changes were needed in terms of their parents' employment, finances, material possessions, access to counselling and behaviour. Only two children in the study did not want to go home.

Contact with social workers

Children in several studies cited irregular or reactive visits from social workers, difficulties in accessing them, and instances of cancelled appointments (Cashmore and Paxman, 1996; Smith *et al.*, 1999; Ward, 2000; Wilson and Conroy, 1999). Some children wanted more visits, others wanted less; they were also disappointed in the lack of continuity in social workers. Reinforcing the importance of relationship, some expressed significant dissatisfaction with their worker:

> He takes no interest whatsoever. He never rings back, he never calls me. He's never in his office when I try to contact him. He will say he will ring at a certain time and then never does. He takes absolutely no interest. I've never known him ring me. He's the worst social worker I've had. (Baldry and Kemmis, 1998, p.38)

In the UK kinship care study, frequent changes in social worker undermined the children's confidence in them:

> I have had 5 social workers and the last one doesn't know nothing about me.

> Has the wrong notes, not helpful and a bit dopey.

> I get used to one social worker and confide in them, and then they say they are going. One I met once. (Doolan *et al.*, 2004, p.39)

Children in Smith *et al.*'s (1999) New Zealand study were confused about the roles of the professionals involved in their care, most did not know who their social worker was and several did not have a social worker. For some children, however, their relationships with caseworkers were positive, although it could take time for these understandings to develop, as this quote from a small qualitative study of young people who had experienced being in care illustrates:

> You know, she (the social worker) was good to me, but I suppose I had to grow up to realise that people were trying to help. And she was definitely out there for me. If I wanted something, she was there for me. (Yates, 2001, p.161)

The contact young people in Cashmore and Paxman's (1996) study had with district officers received mixed responses: for some it was good, for others it was inconsistent. The young people indicated that they would have liked to have been asked about the care they were receiving and for action to be taken when they were not happy. Half of them had someone to confide in (usually the district officer), half of them did not. Many feared 'not being listened to or believed', or reprisals if they spoke out about issues that concerned them (p.47). By contrast, children in Delfabbro *et al.*'s (2002) study thought their caseworkers were 'willing to listen' and were helpful and caring.

Children in Munro's (2001) study placed great importance on their relationship with their social worker, who at best was seen as an ally. Constant changes in social worker, however, left children feeling neglected; appointments that were not kept and irregular reviews made children feel helpless and as if they were 'low priority'. Other research indicates that children want 'a more emotional, empathetic level of interaction' – professional intervention can appear to be 'robotic' (Butler and Williamson, cited in Munro, 2001, p.131).

Involving children and young people in the decision-making process can make a positive contribution to their experiences of out-of-home care and benefit their growth and development in the longer term. A persistent theme throughout the literature is the need for better access to information and better communication between caregivers and children, caregivers and parents, caregivers and social service professionals, and children and social workers. Listening to the voices of children who are or have been in care can alert us to ways in which caregivers and other professionals can either ameliorate or exacerbate the problems that bring them into the child protection system. If we ask them, children will tell us of their concerns and their experiences. It is then up to us to look at how this may influence our practice with them.

Working with children's cultures

Being adults and being more familiar with adult cultures, workers may feel more comfortable working with adults to resolve child care and protection concerns. Despite child protection work being essentially child-focused, somewhat paradoxically the child can get lost in child protection investigations that are dominated by discussions and decision-making between adults. For the same reasons that it is important to hear children's voices in research, it is important to listen to their voices in practice. Perhaps inevitably, given the relative powerlessness of children, power imbalances become immediately apparent (Kroll, 1995) and have to be worked through. According to Kroll there are a number of issues that confront the worker who wants to develop child-centred practice:

- How do we find ways of talking to children? And a related question – what knowledge, background and skill do we need?

- How do we make sure we have time available to listen to children and how do we clear our minds of the busy schedule, the next appointment, and all the other things other people have said about the child?

- How do we build relationships with children that reflect real connections, despite the fact we may be restricted to a few sessions?

- How do we balance both the worker's need to remain focused and the child's contribution by allowing freedom of direction?

- How do we avoid imposing our views on the child? This is particularly complicated when engaging with children is perceived as 'leading the witness'.

- How can the child's voice impact on the understanding and process of the work?

Even though systems of child welfare internationally reinforce the need for workers to work in partnership with family, including children, work continues to remain largely adult-focused. Kroll (1994) suggests that to avoid feelings of helplessness and hopelessness workers may have a tendency to keep their distance from children. Certainly children's stories of loss, rejection, abuse and neglect can be painfully tragic and can cut to the heart of a caring worker. This is not helped by the gnawing awareness that options are often limited and solutions barely good enough. Hampered by a lack of time and expertise it would be easy to understand if workers chose to focus their attention on one-step-distanced discussions with parents or other adults. Nevertheless, practice is strengthened by direct work with children and finding 'methods of communication that enable children to demonstrate their competence' (Thomas and O'Kane, 2000, p.819) becomes part of the challenge.

A 'starter kit' for practice with children

Kroll's (1995) 'starter kit' for practice with children provides some good ideas for getting alongside children and developing a package of knowledge, skills and resources to work effectively with them. The package makes one aware of the need to develop a child-centred philosophy that has respect for children and positions them alongside adults. Having a child-centred philosophy also includes becoming familiar with children's cultures – spending time with children, talking to them, and taking opportunities to see them living their day-to-day lives. The package also advocates knowing more about the theories and research that help to understand the world of a child – and in particular from the perspective of the child. For example, a good knowledge of attachment theory is essential when working with children. Understanding attachment and its impact on resilience forces a worker to interrogate critically the need for removing a child from home, and be acutely aware of the dangers of placement change once there. Concomitant with this is a sound knowledge of the processes of separation and loss and the importance of childhood friendships. From an adult perspective it may seem easy for a child to 'make new friends'. However, as research suggests, children do not see this so straightforwardly and deeply feel the transience of friendships (Sanders, 2004).

Building a repertoire of skills to work with children is important. This involves getting used to feeling a bit silly, working with make-believe and being comfortable with play. Kroll urges us to develop the art of 'being' rather than 'doing', and to avoid the inclination to fix, reassure and write things down.

Finally Kroll's starter kit also includes the systems of worker support, supervision and training. Because listening to children's stories can be both painful and traumatic, having supervision support is an important component of the package. Even experienced workers can feel deskilled and uncertain when stepping into childhood cultures – it's like stepping into any other culture that is unfamiliar. Having said that, children's cultures are rich in their meaning-making. Understanding them helps us to know when processes are helping children and when they cause them harm. Above all they help us to explore and develop culturally responsive practices that better meet their needs.

The United Nations Convention on the Rights of the Child (UNCROC) stresses 'the continuum between child rights and child betterment' (Knutsson, 1999, p.137). While children are recognised as dependent, they are also acknowledged as having the capacity to participate fully in decisions that affect them. In the end, working to understand the nature of children's cultures, listening to what they say and ensuring they are involved in the creation of child-focused service interventions not only will support their rights but also have the potential to contribute to the betterment of children in a meaningful way.

Chapter 5

Family cultures and protecting children

We noted in Chapter 1 that people identify with multiple cultures which also overlap and relate to each other. Children's cultures are embedded within the collective cultures of their family groups. Families provide us with an early set of signposts that help us understand our world. Like road signs, they tell us when it's safe to proceed and when we should exercise caution. They suggest ways of responding to others and they influence the way we think and what we do. They signpost our cultural landscape. From the outside they can appear idiosyncratic and complex. From the inside they appear normal and understandable. As unique as we are in our views of the world, so are the families from which we originate. Understanding the cultural landscape of a family is a complicated assignment but necessary if we are to provide helpful interventions in child protection work.

When working across cultural groups so much depends on how the worker comes across to the family and whether the family believes that they are being understood. Families have their own communication patterns, organisational systems and their own ways of responding to the world. In this chapter we will look at the nature of family systems and the ways in which families have changed over time. Building relationships with families relies on the workers' ability to understand complex systems and their capacity to mobilise the families' cultural strengths toward positive change. We look therefore at ways in which workers can enhance their practice with families by understanding a range of cultural constructs that have the potential to drive family thinking. However, notwithstanding these insights there is no question that cultural misinterpretation confounds practice. People who work with families across cultures will be familiar with that sinking feeling of being lost in translation with barriers to meaning making the cultural signposts just too difficult to read. In these situations alternative ways of thinking about meaning need to be found and we end the chapter by presenting a simple model of supervision that may help workers navigate their way across cultural landscapes. But first, a word or two about families.

Families and family diversity

Family is thought of as 'one of the great, enduring institutions of organized human life…persist[ing] over history across extremely different kinds of society and culture' (Archard, 2003, p.65). The ideal image of the family is of a harmonious and safe entity consisting of married parents and biological children (Anderson and Sabatelli, 2003). However, there is abundant evidence that family forms have changed dramatically over the last few decades (Anderson and Sabatelli, 2003; Carling, 2002; Wise, 2003; Zastrow and Kirst-Ashman, 2004). As well as diversity in family forms, there is increasing diversity in the ethnic identity of people in partnerships.

No longer is the ideal image of family relevant to many in our societies. Archard (2003) suggests that there have been two broad changes in family form over time. The first relates to a shift from marriage as a form of strategic alliance to marriage based on love and compatibility. The second broad change is the move from family being considered a part of the public sphere to it being seen in contemporary times as firmly embedded in the private sphere. New family forms include step-parent, same-sex and single-parent families. While new forms of family have developed, Carling (2002) argues that they have not replaced the long-established institution of marriage.

A number of reasons are given for the change in family forms including increasing economic independence of women, greater acceptance of same-sex relationships, differing expectations of the role of marriage partnerships in achieving personal fulfilment and greater societal acceptance of divorce (Archard, 2003; Carling, 2002; Cherlin, 1992). However, Featherstone (2004, p.19) cautions against drawing a link between this reasoning and 'a deterioration in the quality of family life, particularly for children'.

The meaning attributed to family is therefore fluid, and is dependent on who is doing the defining. As Herbert and Harper-Dorton (2002, p.46) state, 'what we believe about families shapes how we work with families'. While families are diverse in terms of form and ethnicity and meanings attributed to the term vary, a number of features of families can be identified.

Features of families

A family can be thought of as a system that is multi-layered and therefore structurally complicated. Theorists who perceive the family as a system advocate a definition of the family along two key attributes – structure and tasks. *Family structure* relates to family composition and arrangement, that is, 'the unique set of rules governing the patterns of interaction' (Anderson and Sabatelli, 2003, p.6). Family structure is considered to consist of a number of properties identified as wholeness, organisational complexity, interdependence and strategies and rules (Anderson and Sabatelli, 2003).

Wholeness refers to the idea that the family system consists of a number of individuals who together form a group. System approaches recognise the family as consisting of a number of relationships and it is these relationships which tell us more about family dynamics than a focus on individual members would. Worden (2003, p.74) argues that this approach 'places individual behaviour within the greater family context and thus avoids viewing pathology within any one family member'.

Families are *organisationally complex* in that the family system is multi-levelled and consists of subsystems which support family functioning. Three key family subsystems are considered to be:

> the spouse subsystem (the primary concern is each person's role as a part of a couple), parental subsystem (the focus is on the leadership role which is child-focused) and the sibling subsystem (the focus is on the children's private system where they learn to relate to one another and experiment wiithout parental interference). (Crichton-Hill 2004, p.148)

The property of *interdependence* recognises that individuals and subsystems are dependent on one another and influenced by one another. Issues affecting one person in the family, therefore, affect all others.

Strategies and rules govern how family members interact with one another and are essential as the family carries out its tasks. *Family tasks* relate to family responsibilities towards each other and society. Families usually have some mutual history and experience a shared future, experience some level of emotional connection to one another and are focused on meeting both individual and family group needs (Anderson and Sabatelli, 2003). Families are seen as having responsibility for the social, emotional and physical well-being of both children and adults. How these responsibility tasks are met is dependent on the ages and stages of family members. Hence, providing for the social, emotional and physical well-being of a new-born baby requires a different approach to providing for the well-being of an adolescent. This is known as a developmental approach (Bell and Wilson, 2003).

Competent child protection practice with families requires a broad range of skills and knowledge. However, we would argue that a fundamental starting point is the basic recognition and appreciation that families are diverse. This diversity is the result of contextual factors including, but not excluded to, ethnic identity, class, language of choice, health, geographical location, household composition and social and community supports (Munford and Sanders, 1999). Family context also includes societal values about 'what makes a good mother or father, about how sons and daughters should behave, and about what kinds of relationship should exist between husbands and wives' (McLennan *et al.*, 2004, p.82). These are all aspects of cultural thinking that shape the way we think about and behave toward families. Furthermore, families, within themselves, are not homogeneous and therefore 'multiple diverse cultures, with varying ideas about role, membership and structure can exist in one family system...' (Crichton-Hill, 2004, p.147). Additionally, all families will have particular ways in which meaning is given to experiences and in how communication with one another occurs. These are complex areas to tackle when working through issues of child care and protection. Understanding processes of family communication can help.

Communication

Communication has been identified as the process where a person, through the use of signs and symbols, conveys meaning (Koerner and Fitzpatrick, 2002; Reder and Duncan, 2003). The process is reliant on two abilities: the practical and linguistic ability to send and receive information, and the ability to attribute meaning to the message. Successful communication encounters occur when the receiver understands the meaning of the information in the way the sender intended.

Cultural identity and context will have an influence on the way information is transmitted and the way in which it is received. Additionally, 'past experience of a similar issue may sensitize the message receiver to subtle aspects of it or, conversely, revoke stressful emotions and a tendency to dissociate from (or "block out") emotive aspects' (Reder and Duncan, 2003, p.90). This adds to the communication style of the sender and receiver. In encounters with families there will be a number of styles of communication present including the particular communication style of the child protection worker. In addition, families entering into the child protection process will probably experience a range of emotions which may affect their ability to communicate successfully. Moreover, the ability of the child protection worker to communicate will be affected by a range of factors including their personal cultural identity and context, both personal and professional. It is hardly surprising, given the emotive topic of child abuse, that the process of communication between child protection practitioners and families can be fraught with difficulty.

Hwa-Froelich and Vigil (2004), in their examination of how communication is influenced by culture, propose three key areas where differences in cultural thinking and communication may occur: *responsibility relationships, interpersonal relationships* and *risk management*. Although they apply to culture more generally, the areas can be used to explain differences in meaning-making and communication in families and have the potential to contribute to practice enhancement.

Enhancing work with families

Despite the multi-layered complexity of families and their cultural processes, it is important to note that it is, indeed, possible to have successful practice outcomes that reflect the harnessing of cultural strengths. If we understand cultural thinking and the family's associated processes of communication we can incorporate these ideas into practice strategies.

Responsibility relationships

Ideas about responsibility can vary between families and are dependent on the values and beliefs surrounding interpersonal relationships. Hofstede (1984) conceptualises this as a continuum ranging from individual responsibility orientation to collective responsibility orientation. Families who identify generally with individual responsibility may be termed *independent* (self-supporting) while those subscribing to collective (dependent on others) responsibility may be described as *interdependent.*

In families with an individual or independent orientation children are viewed as being able to take care of their own needs and are socialised in order to achieve this outcome. Praise is more likely to be given for tasks that are achieved individually (Hwa-Froelich and Vigil, 2004). Concepts that are considered important include emotional independence, autonomy and rights to privacy. For example, a family with an individual or independent orientation may be less likely to want to involve extended family members in the child protection process and may believe the child protection organisation has no right to be involved with family business. They may be affronted at what they perceive to be an interference in their basic human rights and may move quickly to an adversarial and/or litigious response.

In families with a collective or interdependent orientation families view responsibility as reciprocal and so family members are responsible for each other. Here definition of family is often extended beyond immediate nuclear family members to include aunts, uncles, cousins and grandparents. Important concepts to families with this orientation include group solidarity, sharing of duties and obligations and emotional dependence. Protective services can sometimes be frustrated when, for example, immigrant families send resources back to family in their home country when they may be struggling themselves to manage in their adopted home. Insight into cultural notions of collective responsibility can help a worker to work with the family in these circumstances.

Families with a collective or interdependent orientation may be more receptive to the involvement of extended family. However, it is important to remember that these orientations are not homogeneous categorisations. Each family will be different and stereotyping them to a particular orientation has just as much potential to create miscommunications when working across cultural groups. Rather, the orientations are presented to illustrate different ways of thinking about the world and how the family system may function in relation to that world. Hence, families reflecting an individual or independent orientation may indeed welcome extended family support, while families relating to a collective or independent orientation may not. What is important is that the worker understands the potential for responsibility relationships to influence cultural thinking and how it may, or may not, apply to this particular family.

Interpersonal relationships

Hofstede (1984) suggest that one dimension of social culture is power distance. This refers 'to the vertical stratification of a society where individuals are accorded different levels of importance and status' (Macnamara, 2004, p.323). Within cultural groupings people may be assigned a level of social status influenced by a number of variables such as age, financial wealth, achievements and employment role. Similarly, in family systems individuals will be perceived as having status and therefore power in relation to family functioning.

Hwa-Froelich and Vigil (2004) suggest that people with low power distance relationships are likely to view status inequalities negatively and view those with status as equal to themselves. This orientation lends itself to communication that is direct, but respectful and influenced by a rule of politeness which may result in the use of 'indirect directions and questions' (Hwa-Froelich and Vigil, 2004, p.110).

Accordingly, the writers propose, parents who subscribe to this orientation are likely to communicate with their children in an easy and informal way. Conversely, people with high power distance relationships are very aware of inequalities in relationships. Those who have high power are likely to expect respectful behaviour towards them in communication and in other aspects of family functioning. Parents perceived as holding high power distance in relation to others are likely to use very direct and explicit communication with their children.

Child protection practitioners (depending on their own cultural identity) may perceive parents with high power distance relationships as authoritarian, demanding and unloving. However, things are rarely that straightforward. There are differences between authoritarian and authoritative parenting styles. An authoritarian parenting style can be described as parenting which involves a high level of control over children and a low level of acceptance. Alternatively, 'authoritative parenting is characterised by high levels of both acceptance and control...' (Wise, 2003, p.10). This cautions us against quick assumptions about the way in which the family functions.

Risk management

Families have different strategies for coping with uncertainty and challenge, and will have different cultures of risk-taking. This risk management area is particularly relevant to child protection practice, the nature of which is both challenging and anxiety provoking for families. Hofstede (1984) identified this dimension of social culture as uncertainty avoidance and proposed a continuum of responses from weak uncertainty avoidance to strong uncertainty avoidance. Put simply, some families may be more prepared to foster risk-taking, and some less so. In its application to families, weak uncertainty avoidance characterises responses to challenges and risk-taking as those people who are willing to take risks. Parents who employ this kind of response are likely to socialise children 'to question, take risks, explore, and be creative' (Hwa-Froelich and Vigil, 2004, p.112). Conversely, the orientation to strong uncertainty avoidance (i.e. being risk-averse) represents families who find uncertainty and challenge threatening and uncomfortable. Children from families of this orientation are socialised to do as they are told without challenge and questioning and to steer clear of making mistakes. Children learn through the process of demonstration, the hope of this technique being that by the time the child attempts the task they will be less likely to make an error.

Child protection practitioners who lean towards a weak uncertainty avoidance orientation themselves are likely to be less directive and explicit in their communication with families. They may ask questions and implicitly make suggestions. However, for families who have strong uncertainty avoidance and prefer explicit direction this approach may well be confusing. Consider the situation where the child protection practitioner arranges a family meeting to discuss temporary placement of a child with extended family members. The child protection practitioner (weak uncertainty avoidance) facilitates the meeting in a relaxed way, with few direct questions, in an attempt to engage the family in collaborative decision-making. The family (strong uncertainty avoidance) may not be sure of how they should respond as they are unaware of the worker's expectations. The result is a family whose awkwardness escalates as they fear making a mistake, resulting in lower levels of verbal and non-verbal interaction; ultimately no information is communicated as to the family's opinions. The worker may then see this as the family abdicating their responsibilities, depending on the worker's orientation.

Holland (2000), in her study of child protection assessment practices, discovered that assessment decision-making was strongly influenced by evidence gleaned from verbal interactions with parents. Holland found that social workers perceived parents who were articulate as better able to perform well in assessments. Parents who were inarticulate were perceived as passive and uncooperative, translated by the social worker as representing a lack of insight. Holland identifies the potential for workers to become frustrated when they are unable to elicit information from parents upon which they can 'form a plausible explanation' (p.156) for the abuse issue. While it has long been appreciated that workers need to check carefully the plausibility of any explanation, parental communication styles must not be allowed to influence the assessment unfairly.

Practice-enhancing techniques

Asking families what they find helpful in child care and protection work is important to the enhancement of culturally responsive practice. Parents have identified a number of child protection practitioner characteristics found to make intervention more helpful (Dale, 2004). In relation to practitioner style, Dale found that families valued supportiveness, listening skills, skills in encouraging collaboration, being 'matter of fact' and 'being human' (p.149) – in essence the worker's capacity to be empathic. Empathy has long been considered to be a primary and necessary feature of successful social work practice. Not surprisingly, families wish also to be respected and to be valued as people rather than be labelled as dysfunctional or as a diagnosis (Blue-Banning *et al.*, 2004). In order to hear the family, the worker needs to be able to listen. One way of developing listening skills is to talk less, and to focus on learning through discussion.

Dale (2004) also found that parents wanted to know how decisions in child protection cases were made. As Dale states, 'parents require greater clarity, consistency and transparency in these areas of decision-making' (p.152). The child protection worker therefore has an obligation to be honest and clear in their discussions with families.

Preparing well for their interactions with families also enhances practice. This includes identifying as much information as possible about the cultural identity of the family. Hwa-Froelich and Vigil (2004) suggest that practitioners should have discussions with the family prior to carrying out a formal assessment process. Before an assessment can be done the worker needs to know more about the family's cultural constructs, and these discussions then enable assessment with the family to be balanced alongside other information that has been gathered (Holland, 2000). This approach reduces the likelihood of labelling negatively and unfairly as a result of verbal communication alone.

Other authors promote the use of a *strengths approach* with families (Lee, 2003; Saleebey, 1992; Weick and Saleebey, 1995). The strengths approach essentially attempts to view families as having strengths and potential which can be used to deal with the issues that confront them. As Weick and Saleebey (1995, p.147) aptly state: 'We cannot know, at the outset, the upper limits of any family's potential. We cannot deny the reality and possibility of any family's aspirations.' This is particularly relevant when working across diverse cultural groups since it supports the notion that cultural constructs can be also harnessed as strengths rather than being perceived as problems.

Cultural supervision as an enhancer of practice

Because child care and protection workers make some of the most difficult decisions that the state has to make, and because these are often made in the context of ambiguity and conflicting cultural values, the need for good supervision is of central importance. Cultural miscommunications and misunderstandings will inevitably occur, not only between the worker and the family, but at times also between the worker and the supervisor. Whenever differences in cultural thinking occur the potential exists for people to miss each other, get stuck and be unable to move forward. At times like this an alternative process of supervision that focuses specifically on cultural constructs may help them to navigate cultural territories. We now present a simple model that helps to explore complex and multi-faceted aspects of cultural identity in supervision.

Culture and practice in supervision

Because of the demanding nature of child care and protection work and the domination of risk and safety discourses, issues of culture can become an afterthought in child protection supervision. As discussed in Chapter 3, the child protection environment is one characterised by many pressures and in this context a focus on administrative aspects of child protection work becomes a reality for busy workers and their supervisors. However, if issues of cultural identity are not adequately considered, families will not be as well served by child protection practitioners, and practitioners will not have the opportunity to consider the impact of their cultural identity and biases in their practice.

Supervision has been conceptualised as consisting of three facets which are interrelated: supervisor, child protection practitioner and child or family. These three facets of the supervisory system are interdependent, and so the supervisory process influences the work with families and vice versa. Additionally, each facet brings to the supervisory process its unique cultural identities. The culturally responsive supervision model described below encourages discussion regarding these identities and their impact on practice.

The model is based on a number of principles. First, problems with cultural miscommunication and misunderstanding can be found in different locations – within the family, between the family and the worker, within the worker, between the worker and the supervisor, between the supervisor and the family. Second, there are a number of critical areas that need to be explored to facilitate specific areas of cultural miscommunication. Third, cultural collisions can occur early on in a relationship or when a relationship is well established. Sometimes the tendency for a worker to believe that they 'know the family better than they know themselves' can present barriers to understanding more complex levels of difference. Moreover, workers and supervisors who know each other well may have common assumptions about the work and may be unused to examining critically the underpinning cultural assumptions of each other. The importance of exploring the cultural components has implications therefore for the duration of the supervisory relationship. The final principle is that reciprocity of understanding is necessary in any cross-cultural relationship requiring also an exploration of the *dynamic* of the supervisory relationship rather than being confined to an examination of one person's individual awareness. This principle recognises that supervision is relational and therefore 'knowledge and understanding emerge from the supervisee/supervisor reciprocal engagements and from their collaborative efforts to interpret the meanings of the supervisee/supervisor interactive process as it relates to supervisee/client narratives' (Ringel, 2001, pp.171–2).

Influenced by the literature, the model (shown in Figure 5.1) proposes what we consider to be four critical areas to consider when exploring cultural influences in practice: power, difference, connectedness and meaning. Power and difference are considered to be prerequisite areas that provide the context to understanding the other two quadrants, connectedness and meaning.

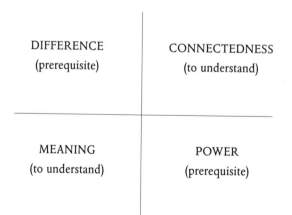

DIFFERENCE
(prerequisite)

CONNECTEDNESS
(to understand)

MEANING
(to understand)

POWER
(prerequisite)

Figure 5.1: Cultural model of supervision

Before further examination of the model, it is important to note that exploration of the quadrants is likely to result in the reciprocal sharing of personal information and that, as such, a high degree of trust is required between the worker and the supervisor. It is not a model of supervision that is 'done to' the worker, nor is it presented as a means of ascertaining worker competence. It is designed to help both worker and supervisor understand and think their way through difficult cultural ideas that are likely to be deeply imbedded in the practice of both the worker and the supervisor. Using the model transparently will help to ensure that inappropriate or personally intrusive practice is avoided.

Exploration of the difference quadrant

An exploration of the quadrants provides an opportunity to explore the cultural dynamics that characterise practice relationships, including the supervisory relationship. Leong and Wagner (1994) propose that difficulties arise in cross-cultural supervisory relationships when cultural issues are not discussed and potentially result in a distorting of the supervisory relationship. Exploration of the difference quadrant allows the worker and supervisor to explore the nature of difference and how it emerges as an issue within the particular practice relationships surrounding the family. Hence, various relationship configurations will be examined: worker and family, worker and supervisor, and so on.

The quadrant encourages discussion relating to both difference and sameness within the relationship configurations. What are some of the advantages and disadvantages of sameness? What are the advantages and disadvantages of difference? How do the workers see themselves as different from the family, and how do they see them as the same? How is this difference and sameness operating in the relationship dynamic? How do experiences of oppression resonate across the relationship configurations – for example racism, sexism, ageism and so forth? How has oppression impacted on life chances? And how do the family's strategies for dealing with oppression resonate across the relationship configurations? Finally, how has practice changed as a result of awareness of oppression? As worker and supervisor explore the quadrants they should maintain a focus on child care and protection which will help them, in turn, to focus the issues on practice and ways of moving forward.

Exploration of the power quadrant

Power is not only an inherent component of child protection practice but is also inextricably linked to the ways in which relationships are perceived across cultures. Practitioners have power in relation to their 'knowledge and expertise; access to resources; statutory powers; and influence over individuals, agencies and so on' (Thompson and British Association of Social Workers, 2001, p.138). Power may potentially be employed in practice in such a way that the worker becomes an oppressor through ignoring differences and conceptualising families as the same as the worker. To a degree this resonates with the supervisor/worker relationship. The supervisor holds positional power within the organisation and may also hold power in relation to experience and knowledge. Hence the supervisor may be perceived as 'expert' by the worker while the worker may be perceived as 'expert' by the family. It is important to note here that power doesn't only operate one way – professional power over family power. If a worker feels culturally ill at ease and powerless in the face of a closely knit and powerful family group they may feel reluctant to give effect to their child protection statutory powers. These feelings need to be explored if the child is to remain safe.

The power quadrant encourages discussion about the nature of power and powerlessness across the relationship configurations; for example, position power, personal power, cultural power. How is power influencing the processes of the work and the ways in which decisions are being made? What structural inequalities exist and do they impact on the work? How can structural inequalities be responded to? How do the organisational structure and power impact on professional conduct and capacity to connect with the family? How are power and powerlessness mirrored across the relationship configurations? Who has control over decision-making processes?

Exploration of the connectedness quadrant

The extent of the discussion in each of the quadrant areas will be influenced by the relationship between supervisor and practitioner. It is most likely that in a relationship which is open and enabling and within a secure environment workers will feel free to explore the ways in which their own personal and professional selves intersect with cultural thinking. Meaning connections are enhanced by the establishment of respect and rapport between people. The concept of respect is important to people and can be described as 'an internal orientation to the world...and...as a set of overt behaviors' (Hays, 2001, p.73). Rapport is enhanced when one does not presume that the other's cultural identity is known and understood.

The elements of rapport and respect are important when considering issues of connectedness. Understanding how dependence, interdependence and separateness are perceived is important when working with diverse cultural groups. How do relationship responsibilities work across the relationship configurations? How does connectedness resonate with notions of familial duty and loyalty? How does the family demonstrate connectedness or separateness in family relationships? How does the worker demonstrate connectedness or separateness in family relationships? What are the elements of connectedness between the worker and the family? Does the family seek a connection with the worker? How does the concept of connectedness help in the understanding of cultural difference? How is connectedness limited or enhanced in the context of power and difference?

Exploration of the meaning quadrant

As discussed in this chapter and elsewhere in the book, when it comes down to actually understanding what people mean it is often much, much harder than we think it will be. When communication crosses cultural boundaries things can become complicated and misunderstandings are likely to occur. This supports the notion that meaning barriers exist between all people and working our way through them is a daily task.

How people ascribe meaning to their experiences will depend on how they see themselves relating to the world around them. Meaning therefore cannot be disconnected from the sets of beliefs and values that we all hold and that drive the way we think and act. How does meaning-making help this particular family confront the difficulties ahead of them? How do they make sense of what has happened? Is this different from the way in which the worker makes sense of it? What is the importance of objective and subjective meaning? How do the meanings we ascribe influence our attitudes toward difference, power and connectedness?

It is also important to consider how the prerequisite areas of power and difference impact on the meanings and beliefs held by workers within the agency and the values of the agency itself. What does the organisation believe (ascribed meaning) is the best way to manage issues of cultural difference?

Supervision provides an opportunity to explore alternative explanations and interventions for child protection practice. We argue that by proactively putting culture on the supervision agenda we have an opportunity to develop more complex understanding of how culture and diversity influence relationship configurations within and across systems.

The concept of partnership is frequently mentioned in the child protection literature. For effective child protection practice, partnerships need to be developed across this range of configurations including child, family, parent, agency and professional systems. However, true partnership is only possible if workers are able to recognise the diverse complexity of family systems and if they seek to understand how cultural meanings shape the way practice develops. Models of supervision such as the one described in this chapter are just one way of digging a little deeper in the search for solutions.

Chapter 6

Cultures of risk, offending and good lives

Having looked at children and families in Chapters 4 and 5, we now turn to another group whose behaviour and processes of cultural thinking also impact on child care and protection work: the sexual offender. This group contributes another piece to the abuse jigsaw and knowledge of offending cultures is important for any worker practising with children and families in the child protection field.

It has become increasingly clear that it is possible to reduce criminal behaviour by treating or rehabilitating offenders rather than simply punishing them (Andrews and Bonta, 1998; Gendreau and Andrews, 1990; Hollin, 1999). The rehabilitation perspective rests on a number of important assumptions about crime and the characteristics of offenders. First, it assumes that crime is caused by distinct patterns of social and psychological factors that increase the chances that a given individual will break the law. Second, it assumes that targeting these factors will decrease reoffending rates. Third, it assumes that individuals vary in their predisposition to commit deviant acts and this should be taken into account when planning rehabilitation programmes. In other words, treatment should be tailored to meet each offender's unique needs (Ogloff and Davis, 2004). Following from this it acknowledges that a one-size-fits-all treatment perspective is unlikely to be of much value when working with offenders.

A careful reading of the correctional literature reveals that there are two general models of offender rehabilitation, each possessing a unique set of assumptions about the causes of crime, the values underpinning rehabilitation, and the best way to help individuals to desist from further offending.

The first supports a culture of *risk management*, where the primary aim is to make the community a safer place through reducing offenders' risk factors. The relationship between offenders' welfare or quality of life and recidivism rates is an instrumental one: it is a means to the end of reduced risk to the community. The core values underlying the risk management model are those of community safety and control, and offenders are typically regarded as deserving less consideration and respect than non-offenders.

In contrast, the *enhancement* model is directly concerned with equipping individuals with the capabilities necessary to live better lives, thereby reducing the likelihood of them committing further criminal actions. By focusing on providing offenders with the necessary conditions (for example, skills, values, opportunities, and social supports) for meeting their needs in more adaptive ways, the assumption is that they will then be less likely to harm themselves and others. In this model, the primary end or goal is not the reduction of crime, although it is argued that this will reliably follow from individual well-being. The cultural values underlying the enhancement model are humanistic and strongly advocate for offenders' right to be treated with compassion and respect while appreciating that their behaviour has resulted in harm to others. The enhancement model is more widely accepted in clinical psychology and its presence in corrections has occurred through the incorporation of clinical psychological models into work with offenders. Nevertheless, the risk management model has tended to dominate correctional psychology and offender rehabilitation policy (see Andrews and Bonta, 1998; Ashford, Sales and Reid, 2001; Garland, 2001).

In Chapter 1 we defined *culture* as a dynamic system consisting of a combination of interrelated components that work coherently together to regulate human behaviour. In sum, culture is something that greatly influences how we think, what we do and how we do it, including practices, competencies, ideas, symbols, values, norms, institutions, goals, constitutive rules, artefacts and modifications of the physical environment. The markedly different views of offender rehabilitation briefly described above constitute distinct treatment cultures and, as such, are associated with diverse attitudes, values and ideas concerning the causes of offending, the status of offenders, and the primary aim of interventions. Clearly the assumptions underlying each of these offending or treatment cultures colours the way that clinicians, policy makers and social service workers more generally regard both offenders and their treatment. Less obviously, they also bias the way offenders regard themselves. For example, whether individuals view themselves as essentially bearers of risk or as moral agents trying to make their way in the world by building 'good' lives makes a huge difference to their commitment to the treatment process.

In this chapter we examine two contrasting approaches to the rehabilitation of offenders, the risk–need–responsivity (RNR) model and the good lives model (GLM). The RNR model is an example of a risk management perspective where the aim in treating offenders is to reduce and/or manage their level of risk to the community. The GLM is an example of an enhancement or strength-based approach where the aim is to enhance the well-being of offenders alongside the management of risk. In other words, the GLM has the twin focus of risk management and goods promotion (explained more fully on p.98). The GLM provides a new way of looking at offender work, and explores the needs of the offender in the context of a set of meaning-making relationships that ultimately provide impetus for change.

The RNR model

The RNR model is an example of a rehabilitation theory and as such has a number of assumptions about the causes of crime and the aim of treatment. First, it assumes that the best way to stop a person from committing further offences is to specifically target their cluster of dynamic risk factors (for example, the offender's antisocial attitudes or deviant sexual arousal). Second, the RNR model is based on the (value) commitment to reduce harm to the community through the elimination or management of risk factors. Third, these factors are seen as constituting clinical needs or problems that should be explicitly targeted. Fourth, according to the RNR model, risk assessment drives the treatment process and the offender's assessed level of risk determines how much treatment they actually receive. It is assumed that focusing rehabilitation on dynamic risk factors (or criminogenic needs) will result in lower rates of crime. This is achieved through the reduction or management of psychological and social characteristics found to cause criminal acts and associated with increased offending rates.

Principles of the RNR model

The RNR model is a rather simple one and essentially consists of a list of principles derived from the assumptions outlined above about the nature of offending and the need to focus intervention on risk management. These principles have been clearly formulated by Andrews and Bonta and have been labelled the risk, need, responsivity and professional discretion principles (Andrews and Bonta, 1998). Andrews and Bonta recommend that the principles be used to select treatment targets and guide the way treatment is actually implemented.

First, the *risk* principle simply states that there should be a relationship between offenders' assessed level of risk and the amount of treatment they receive. The assumption is that risk is an approximate marker of clinical need. According to the risk principle, high-risk individuals require a considerable amount of cognitive behavioural treatment from trained and qualified staff over a sustained period of time, probably in the range of 200–300 hours (Ogloff and Davis, 2004). Correspondingly, medium-risk individuals should only receive about 50 hours or so of interventions, while those assessed as low risk need minimal, if any, treatment. Risk can be divided into static and dynamic risk factors. Static risk factors are those characteristics of the individual or their lifestyle that cannot be changed; for example, age at the time of first offence, severity of previous offending or gender. By way of contrast, dynamic risk factors are features of the individual or of their situation that are changeable and therefore suitable targets for treatment. Furthermore, an important assumption is that the severity of risk (whether it is low, medium or high) is likely to be reliably associated with the number of problems exhibited by offenders. For example, individuals assessed as high risk are likely to display a greater number of dynamic risk factors than those viewed as low risk.

Second, the *need* principle states that it is important for workers to only target risk factors that are causally related to reoffending. These are called *criminogenic needs* – that is, dynamic offender characteristics that, when changed, are associated with reduced recidivism rates. Examples of criminogenic needs include offence supportive attitudes (for example distorted thinking processes), impulsiveness, poor problem-solving, substance abuse, high levels of hostility and anger and a tendency to associate with antisocial peers (Andrews and Bonta, 1998). The identification of criminogenic needs is a straightforward process and relies exclusively on the use of statistical methods. What researchers look for are those variables that when reduced or modified in some way, result in lowered reoffending rates. Criminogenic needs are identified through the statistical examination of large data sets and therefore may vary for different types of crimes. Thus criminogenic needs are empirically derived (from the perspective of the RNR model) through what is perceived to be a value-free process. This is seen as a virtue as values are viewed with suspicion by proponents of the RNR model and thought to be essentially arbitrary preferences for certain outcomes or experiences.

According to the RNR model it is imperative to distinguish between criminogenic needs and non-criminogenic needs. *Non-criminogenic* needs are characteristics of the individual or their circumstances that if changed have no direct impact on recidivism rates. Examples of non-criminogenic needs are clinical phenomena such as low self-esteem and mental health problems such as depression or unresolved grief. The important issue to grasp here is that proponents of the RNR model view the explicit targeting of non-criminogenic needs during therapy as discretionary because of the negligible impact any change in these variables have on recidivism rates. For example, setting out to enhance an offender's self-esteem may leave them feeling better about themselves but, according to Andrews and Bonta, will not on its own reduce reoffending rates. In fact, according to some research, targeting such variables may in fact increase individuals' chances of reoffending (Ogloff and Davis, 2004). It is important to note that both criminogenic and non-criminogenic needs are not to be equated with human needs, discussed later in the chapter, but are best viewed as clinical problems.

Third, the *responsivity* principle states that it is essential to take into account individuals' relevant characteristics such as cognitive ability, learning style, ethnicity, gender and values (Andrews and Bonta, 1998) when implementing treatment. In other words, responsivity refers to the extent to which offenders are able to absorb the content of the programme and subsequently change their behaviour; it is a matching principle. The responsivity principle encourages workers to consider the offender's motivation for engaging in thereapy and committing to change and to tailor treatment accordingly. Responsivity as usually understood in the rehabilitation literature is primarily concerned with therapist and therapy features and is, therefore, essentially concerned with adjusting treatment delivery in a way that maximises learning.

Finally, the principle of *professional discretion* states that in some circumstances clinical judgement should override the above principles. This allows for treatment flexibility and innovation under certain circumstances. For example, if a person is extremely distressed after hearing that his wife has left him it may be sensible to spend some time listening to his worries and dealing with the practical issues this event entails rather than simply moving on to the next scheduled phase of treatment. According to Andrews and Bonta, it is critical that the principle of professional discretion is not applied in an overly liberal manner, otherwise the principles of risk and need may be violated.

The implications of the RNR model for assessment and treatment of offenders are quite significant. Focused on preventing reoffending, the model is highly structured, specialist in nature (cognitive-behavioural) and delivered in the correct manner by highly trained staff within an environment that is committed to the ideas of rehabilitation (Andrews and Bonta, 1998; Hollin, 1999; McGuire and Priestly, 1995; Ogloff and Davis, 2004).

There is no question that the RNR model of offender rehabilitation has been a significant achievement and has helped to reduce reoffending rates in correctional psychology. Its success has essentially made it the premier rehabilitation theory and writers have attested to its clinical utility (Ward and Stewart, 2003b). As with any approach, however, it also has its weaknesses. First, treatment decisions are made on the basis of a risk assessment, rather than a consideration of broader human welfare issues. Like most other people, offenders respond to initiatives that indicate a genuine interest in them as people, and they will respond if they think that their lives will be better if they give up crime. Even though their relationship problems may not be directly related to their offending, to ignore them may lead to trouble in the future. Second, basing treatment on risk management assumes that the major aim of rehabilitation is to reduce the chances of harm to the community and that this is best achieved by managing risk. There are two problems with this. Offenders are not necessarily going to be motivated by community safety concerns. While reduction of risk to the community is an excellent social aim it does not translate well into clinical aims when working with individual offenders. What tends to work better is the belief that change will be personally meaningful and satisfying. Focusing on criminogenic needs works on the basis of what offender behaviour requires if it is to be eliminated rather than what behaviours can be promoted or enhanced. Indeed, negative goals like those in this model are extremely difficult to achieve, because they do not specify what should be sought but merely what should be avoided or escaped from (Emmons, 1999).

Basic human need

One of the weaknesses of the RNR model is its lack of attention to human need. Deci and Ryan (2000, p.229) usefully define human needs as 'innate psychological nutriments that are essential for ongoing psychological growth, integrity, and well-being'. *Human needs* are the conditions essential for psychological well-being, which must be met in an appropriate manner for individuals to experience deep satisfaction and happiness. If basic physical, social or psychological human needs are not met then a person is likely to be harmed in some manner; for example, they may suffer physical ill health or lowered levels of psychological well-being. Basic needs require external and internal conditions for their fulfilment – adequate parenting, opportunities to learn and make independent decisions, the possession of skills necessary to establish intimate relationships and so on. There is not much point having a need for relationships if an individual lacks the social skills required to communicate effectively with another person or simply does not have the opportunity to interact with others. The various goods or valued activities that typically comprise a satisfying life (for example, health, knowledge, creativity and friendship) are only possible if basic human needs are being meet (Braybrooke, 1987; Thomson, 1987).

The RNR model also neglects the role of personal identity in the change process. There is evidence from research on the change process in offenders generally, and also from recent therapeutic initiatives in the treatment of intellectually disabled sex offenders, that the formation of a prosocial identity is a necessary condition for desisting from reoffending. The first piece of evidence comes from Shadd Maruna's (2001) research on the self-narratives of offenders who desist from committing further offences. Maruna found that in order to be effectively rehabilitated, individuals need to establish an alternative coherent and prosocial identity. This required the construction of a narrative that made sense of their earlier crimes and experiences of adversity and created a bridge between their undesirable life and new ways of living. Desisting offenders appeared to live their lives according to a *redemption script*, where negative past experiences were reinterpreted as providing a pathway or conduit to the forging of a new identity and more authentic ways of living.

In the sexual offending field, Haaven and Coleman (2000) developed a model for the treatment of developmentally disabled sex offenders based on the construction of a new personal identity. In this model, treatment is based around the distinction between a 'new me' and an 'old me'. The 'old me' constitutes the individual who committed sexual offences and encompasses values, goals, beliefs and ways of living that directly generate offending behaviour. The construction of a 'new me' involves the endorsement of a new set of goals that specify a 'good' life for an individual, that is, a life in which important primary goods are achieved in ways that are socially acceptable and personally fulfilling.

Furthermore, the RNR model does not really address the issue of personal agency. The capacity of individuals to seek meaning and to direct their actions in the light of reason and values constitutes an essential aspect of human functioning, according to research on well-being and self-regulation (Deci and Ryan, 2000; Emmons, 1996, 1999). The presence of conflicting goals and a reduced sense of autonomy are likely to result in lower levels of well-being and higher incidences of psychopathology (Emmons, 1999). The capabilities underpinning the capacity for autonomous functioning (along with other basic human needs and goods) should arguably be instilled in the work with offenders. The conditions and skills constituting autonomy would allow offenders to exercise personal choice in the shaping of their lives and the various components collectively constituting such lives (for example, relationships, work, play, mastery experiences and so forth).

A culture of 'good lives'

Positive psychology is the social work equivalent of a strength-based approach to the study of human behaviour – it focuses on promoting human welfare and building on cultural strengths rather than simply emphasising psychological deficits (Aspinwall and Staudinger, 2003). It has ancient cultural roots and is evident in Aristotle's view that human beings are naturally oriented towards seeking fulfilment of their potentialities and, furthermore, that a fulfilling or flourishing life is only possible if these potentialities are realised (Jorgensen and Nafstad, 2004). It is the perfection of essential human qualities that yields happiness in the sense of psychological well-being or fulfilment. According to Aristotle, human flourishing is not the same thing as a subjective happiness. He argued that a person could be happy in the sense they tend to experience pleasant states but could also be essentially unfulfilled. In other words, these individuals are choosing to live in ways that deny important aspects of their character and needs – they are not striving toward realising their potential as human beings. For example, a hedonist could live a life of pleasure-seeking and neglect their needs for personal growth, autonomy, relatedness, mastery and creativity. The stress on human nature and human flourishing indicates the strong humanistic strand in both social work and positive psychology.

This strength-based approach operates on a number of assumptions about human nature. First, it views human beings as naturally predisposed to seek a number of primary goods that, if achieved, are likely to result in high levels of psychological well-being. Human goods are viewed as objective and tied to certain ways of living that, if pursued, involve the actualisation of potentialities that are distinctively human. These goods all contribute to a happy or fulfilling life but are intrinsically valuable in themselves (for example, related-ness, creativity, physical health and mastery). Primary goods emerge out of basic needs while instrumental or secondary goods provide concrete ways of securing these goods; for example, certain types of work, relationships or language ability. The nature of the primary goods sought by individuals and their weightings are formed in specific cultural contexts and represent indi-viduals' interpretations of interpersonal and social events. This knowledge is clearly influenced by culturally derived beliefs, values and norms (D'Andrade, 1995). The underlying metaphor is that of a complex, dynamic system where the way individuals seek specific human goods impacts on the other goods sought, the environment and, ultimately, the quality of their lives and subsequent levels of well-being.

A critical issue concerns the range and type of goods sought by human beings and what, if any, research evidence there is for these phenomena. Taking into account the findings from a number of disciplines, including anthropology, social science, social policy, psychology, evolutionary theory, practical ethics and philosophical anthropology, we propose that there are at least nine types of primary human goods (see Arnhart, 1998; Aspinwall and Staudinger, 2003; Cummins, 1996; Emmons, 1999; Linley and Josephy, 2004; Murphy, 2001; Nussbaum, 2000; Rasmussen, 1999). In no particular order they are life (including healthy living and functioning), knowledge, excellence in play and work (including mastery experiences), excellence in agency (for example, autonomy and self-directedness), inner peace (freedom from emotional turmoil and stress), friendship (including intimate, romantic and family relationships), community, spirituality (in the broad sense of finding meaning and purpose in life), happiness and creativity. Although this list is comprehensive it is not meant to be exhaustive. It is also possible to divide the primary goods into related but more fine-grained goods. For example, the good of inner peace could be broken down into a number of related goods such as the eight sets of emotional competency skills described by Saarni (1999). These eight emotional competency skills include awareness of one's emotional state, the capacity to identify other people's emotions, the ability to use the emotional vocabulary of one's culture, the capacity to respond empathically to other people and the ability to adjust one's emotional presentation depending on circumstances (Saarni, 1999).

The second assumption underpinning this strength-based approach is that individuals should be understood in an holistic, integrated manner rather than through the pursuit of reductionistic research programmes. A particularly important feature of humans beings is their personal and cultural identity and the subsequent attempts by individuals to construct accounts of their lives that give them purpose and value.

Third, the aim of treatment initiatives guided by positive psychology is to give people the necessary capabilities to live more fulfilling lives rather than simply seek to reduce risk factors or focus on the amelioration of psychological deficits. People are viewed as psychological agents who flourish when able to make their own decisions concerning the direction of their lives provided they possess the necessary skills, capabilities and resources to do so. Human well-being is a self-directed activity and therefore springs from each individual's own choices and effort; it cannot be a result of factors beyond the control of the person in question. Furthermore, the existence of strengths can act as a buffer against the development of psychological problems and disorders.

Fourth, people are viewed as contextually and culturally embedded organisms who depend on each other for the provision of the resources, skills and opportunities to lead worthwhile and satisfying lives. Any attempt to explain or remedy individuals' problems needs to take into account the environment in which they live. Fifth, there is no such thing as the ideal or perfect human life.

Individuals legitimately vary in the weightings they give to particular sets of primary goods and in the way these goods are translated into specific activities and experiences (e.g. types of mastery experiences, kinds of relationship). The emphasis given to the primary kinds and the different ways they are realised will depend on a person's abilities, preferences and life circumstances. Thus the basic goods that comprise human nature cannot be read off like some kind of recipe and combined in the same way for all individuals. Seligman and Csikszentmihalyi (2000, p.5) have provided a nice description of positive psychology that captures most of the elements described above:

> The field of positive psychology at the subjective level is about valued subjective experiences: well-being, contentment, and satisfaction (in the past); hope and optimism (for the future); and flow and happiness (in the present). At the individual level, it is about positive individual traits: the capacity for love and vocation, courage, interpersonal skill, aesthetic sensibility, perseverance, forgiveness, originality, future mindedness, spirituality, high talent, and wisdom. At the group level, it is about the civic virtues and the institutions that move individuals toward better citizenship: responsibility, nurturance, altruism, civility, moderation, tolerance, and work ethic.

An important part of positive psychology is its insistence that human fulfilment emerges from certain types of activities rather than simply the attainment of material goods or social status. The significant activities are those associated with the attainment of primary human goods such as relatedness and creativity. The process of pursuing a vision of a good life is clearly a dynamic and ongoing one; it never ends. A positive psychological approach to understanding human behaviour will always take the dynamic character of human well-being into account and therefore focus on the interaction between subjective experience, character traits and the social, cultural and personal environment of the participants concerned.

The Good Lives Model

The good lives model (GLM) of offender rehabilitation is underpinned by these strength-based concepts. We argue that the GLM is able to clarify the underlying theoretical basis of wellness, well-being and personal identity, and also directly addresses the contextual nature of human functioning. The GLM is an example of a positive psychological approach to the treatment of offenders and shares a number of the core assumptions of this perspective. First, it assumes that, as human beings, offenders are goal-directed organisms who are predisposed to seek a number of primary goods. As noted above, primary goods are states of affairs, states of mind, personal characteristics, activities or experiences that are sought for their own sake and are likely to increase psychological well-being if achieved. Instrumental or secondary goods provide concrete ways and means of securing these goods, for example, certain types of work, relationships or language ability. It is assumed that offending reflects socially unacceptable and often personally frustrating attempts to pursue primary human goods. Second, rehabilitation is a value-laden process and involves a variety of different types of values including prudential values (what is in the best interests of sexual offenders), ethical values (what is in the best interests of community) and epistemic or knowledge-related values (what are our best practice models and methods).

Third, the GLM places critical important on the construction of personal identity and its relationship to sexual offenders' understanding of what constitutes a good life. In our view, individuals' conceptions of themselves directly arises from their basic value commitments (human goods), which are expressed in their daily activities and lifestyle. People acquire a sense of who they are and what really matters from what they do: their actions are suffused with values. What this means for social workers is that it is not enough simply to equip individuals with skills to control or manage their risk factors, it is imperative that they are also give the opportunity to fashion a more adaptive cultural identity, one that bestows a sense of meaning and fulfilment.

Fourth, in our view the concept of good lives should play a major role in determining the form and content of rehabilitation programmes, alongside that of risk management. Thus, a treatment plan needs to incorporate the various primary goods (e.g., relatedness, health, autonomy, creativity, knowledge) and aim to provide the internal and external conditions necessary to secure these goods. This necessitates obtaining an holistic account of an offender's lifestyle leading up to their offending and using this knowledge to help them develop a more viable and explicit good lives plan.

Fifth, one assumption behind the GLM is that human beings are contextually dependent organisms and as such, a rehabilitation plan should always take into account the match between the characteristics of the offender and the likely environments they are likely to be released into. Thus, we argue that the notion of adaptive or coping skills should always be linked to the contexts in which offenders are embedded.

Finally, according to the GLM, a treatment plan needs to be explicitly constructed in the form of a good lives conceptualisation. In other words it should take into account offenders' strengths, primary goods and cultural environments, and should specify exactly what competencies and resources are required to achieve these goods. An important aspect of this process is respecting offenders' capacity to make certain decisions themselves, and in this sense, accepting their status as autonomous individuals. In the context of offending treatment such decisions are likely to revolve around the weightings of the primary goods and also the specific types of activities utilised to translate the primary goods into an offender's daily routine. For example, the kind of works, education and further training and types of relationships identified and selected.

The GLM

The GLM theory of sexual offender rehabilitation is, therefore, a strength-based approach that embodies a number of the positive psychological principles outlined above. The primary aim of practice is to instil in offenders the knowledge, skills and competencies for them to implement a meaningful and viable good lives plan in the type of environment they will move to post-treatment. The focus is, therefore, on the core ideas of agency, psychological well-being and the opportunity to live a different type of life, one that is likely to provide a viable alternative to a criminal lifestyle (Kekes, 1989; Rapp, 1998; Ward and Stewart, 2003a).

The possibility of constructing and translating conceptions of good lives into actions and concrete ways of living depends crucially on the possession of internal (skills and capabilities) and external conditions (opportunities and supports). The specific form that a conception will take depends on the actual abilities, interests and opportunities of each individual and the weightings they give to specific primary goods. The weightings or priority allocated to specific primary goods is constitutive of an offender's personal identity and spells out the kind of life sought and, related to this, the kind of person they would like to be. For example, an offender who places greater weight on relationships than other primary human goods might seek to work as a community volunteer in a non-risk area of reoffending. The importance of this primary good would be reflected in their self-conception and give their life a sense of dignity and meaning.

However, because human beings naturally seek a range of primary goods or desired states, it is important that all the classes of primary goods are addressed in a conception of good lives; they need to be ordered and coherently related to each other. For example, for the offender who decides to pursue a life characterised by service to the community, a core aspect of their identity will revolve around the primary goods of relatedness and social life. The offender's sense of mastery, self-esteem, perception of autonomy and control will all reflect this overarching good and its associated sub-clusters of goods (e.g. intimacy, caring, honesty). The resulting good lives conceptions should be organised in ways that ensure each primary good has a role to play and can be secured or experienced by the individual concerned. The basic idea is that primary goods function like essential cooking ingredients and all need to be present in some form if a person is to experience high levels of well-being. A conception that is fragmented and lacks coherence is likely to lead to frustration and harm to the individual concerned, as well as a life lacking an overall sense of purpose and meaning (Emmons, 1996). Additionally, a conception of good lives is always dependent on context; there is no such thing as the right kind of life for an individual across every conceivable setting.

The GLM is not unconcerned with risk management. The identification of risk factors alerts workers to problems (obstacles) in the way offenders are seeking to achieve valued or personally satisfying outcomes. Therefore, the identification of risk elements is a critical part of assessment because they flag the existence of problems in the way individuals seek primary human goods. Different categories of risk factors point to problems in the pursuit of different types of human goods. Hence, dynamic risk factors (criminogenic needs) and the GLM can be conceptually related. We believe that offender treatment plans need to be explicitly constructed and based on a culture of good lives. Responses need to take into account offenders' preferences, strengths, primary goods and relevant environments, and need to be based around the constructs of personal identity, primary goods and ways of living.

In this chapter we have examined two quite different approaches to the rehabilitation of offenders. They reflect two different cultures of offender treatment constituting markedly distinct ways of understanding offending behaviour and the best way to prevent people from reoffending. In our opinion, the GLM has taken an important step toward developing sex offender treatment services that respond to human need. Like other approaches described in this book, the GLM is essentially ecological in nature, acknowledging the cultural interdependence of human beings and the need for services that are contextually located.

Chapter 7

Culturally reflexive theory and practice in child protection

Having explored the nature of culture and cultural practice in previous chapters, we now turn to theory. In this chapter we set out to blend theoretical cultures with other forms of cultural thinking about child abuse and its psychological, social, emotional and biological concomitants. Our aim is to construct an holistic theoretical perspective knitted together from ideas prominent in offender cultures and the various cultures constituting the child protection domain (see Chapters 1 and 6).

Theories of offending are cultural resources that spell out the aims of intervention and the nature of therapeutic practices, and instruct practitioners in how to work with abusive individuals and their families. They provide a framework for assessment by noting the difficulties individuals are likely to experience, describing how such problems are interrelated and specifying their psychological, social, biological and cultural causes. They set us on a pathway of understanding and response.

A good case formulation in the child protection arena needs to outline the developmental factors that make individuals vulnerable to committing abuse. In essence, it is a micro-theory designed to explain why a particular child, embedded within a specific social and cultural network, was abused by their caregivers. In order to clarify the abuse story it is necessary to speak about the caregivers and the family's developmental history, cultural background, cultural systems (e.g. child protection services) and current circumstances. The relevant developmental variables will include factors such as inconsistent parenting, cultural dislocation, poverty or being a victim of physical or sexual abuse in the past. These learning events could lead to the formation of destructive attitudes and behaviours that subsequently play a role in the abuse of a child. For example, a parent who was neglected or abused as a child might become insecurely attached (poor parental bonding) and in later life experience intense episodes of loneliness and social rejection causing them to behave in an abusive manner. Another person brought up to consider that feelings are bad could learn to suppress or ignore them. In this situation it is conceivable that a lifetime of emotional neglect could make it difficult for individuals to communicate feelings of distress in a healthy way. The failure to effectively resolve an emotional crisis could be a partial cause of subsequent physical abuse.

From a practice perspective, the presence of different vulnerability factors in different individuals requires the application of distinct therapeutic strategies, or at least the placement of different priorities on existing service responses, depending on the individuals' needs. For example, some individuals may need to acquire relatively greater levels of relationship skills to address relationship difficulties while others would benefit from learning how to manage their moods more effectively. Others require resources that would alleviate the pressures within the family system.

It should be apparent by now that we view theory as an indispensable tool for practitioners as well as researchers. We are also committed to exploring ways in which cultural thinking and theory can be knitted together to provide more culturally responsive practices. Put simply, theories are cultural resources, cognitive tools for solving problems that inevitably confront us as we make our way in the world. We require a wide range of different theories, each performing their own tasks. The fact that we rely on a variety of theories and cultural resources to explain, predict and understand the different environments within which our lives unfold, means that taking the time to stop and explicitly think about theoretical matters is a valuable and practical thing to do.

In our opinion, the issues of theory formation and appraisal have been somewhat neglected by workers in the field, with most current interest centring on risk assessment, classification and treatment efficacy. These are worthy and important topics but all are dependent on underlying aetiological (what causes a problem or disorder) and treatment theories. It is time to expose the assumptions about aetiology residing deep within our current practices and to shed a critical light on the way we think about child abuse and, by implication, provide more compelling justifications for intervention. In short, it is timely to stop and think about why we do what we do, and whether or not it is possible to improve the quality and depth of our thinking about child protection matters.

In this chapter we blend together different theoretical cultures into an holistic framework that we call the culturally reflexive model (CRM) of child protection. The CRM knits together ideas from the sexual offending field and the child protection area to provide practitioners with the conceptual resources to assess and intervene in cases of child abuse. Thus, cultural resources in the form of ideas and practices are drawn from a myriad of distinct, but overlapping, cultures: offender cultures, child cultures and broader social and ecological systems and cultures. Our aim is to help practitioners think in a richer and more systematic way about child protection issues. First, we provide a brief overview of the model and describe some of the underlying assumptions that underpin it. Second, we discuss the nature of theory construction and evaluation in the child protection area and the process of 'theory knitting'. Third, the child protection model is systematically outlined and its application to the child protection area described. In order to illustrate the practice utility of our model we briefly present case examples reflecting one of the four major pathways to child abuse. Finally, the model is evaluated against the theory appraisal criteria formulated earlier in the chapter.

Overview of the culturally reflexive model of child protection practice

In brief, the CRM proposes that there are a number of distinct aetiological pathways that result in the physical assault of a child. Each of these independent pathways is proposed as having at its centre a unique array of factors that cause the problems typically seen in groups of individuals who abuse children and in families within which abuse occurs. In other words, different causal pathways to child abuse will have their own suite of causes derived from varying social experiences and developmental experiences. Caregivers physically assault children for different reasons. We suggest that each set of causes, in conjunction with circumstantial factors, results in abuse. The four clusters of causal factors are:

- physical and maturational factors
- resourcing factors
- historical factors
- social and cultural factors.

Thus in some families the primary causal pathway may be extreme poverty and environmental disadvantage. There may be a lack of adequate nutrition, substandard housing and insufficient resources to respond to the basic needs of the family unit. In this example, the lack of basic resources is hypothesised to create extreme stress within a family and lower the threshold for child abuse. By way of contrast, in another family the causal pathway may be social and cultural factors where past inadequate modelling of conflict resolution skills and good parenting practices may leave individuals without the resources to parent their own children when the time comes. The inability to discipline children or simply to deal effectively with the inevitable conflicts of family life could result in child abuse. The basic idea is that intervening effectively with abusive families requires competent assessment which, in turn, depends on a good aetiological theory of child abuse. In other words, practice and theory are intimately related.

Different types of theories can be located on the varying professional discourses of child protection workers and in related disciplines such as psychology, correctional services and social work. Furthermore, there are a variety of theoretical cultures within each of these domains. For example, the reigning paradigm in offender rehabilitation theory, the risk–need–responsivity (RNR) model, is an empirically driven strategy for reducing offender risk levels and therefore promoting community safety. This approach contrasts with strength-based models which seek to enhance offenders' abilities to meet their needs in personally satisfying and socially acceptable ways and, by doing so, also to reduce the rates of reoffending. Both approaches have merit and it would be a mistake to base rehabilitation on only one of these perspectives. We argue that rehabilitation should focus both on promoting human goods (providing the offender with the essential ingredients for a 'good' life) as well as reducing/ avoiding risk (see Chapter 6).

The CRM adopts an ecological perspective and states that individuals are embedded in networks of different types of relationships, physical, personal, social and cultural (Germain, 1991). The way people act is a direct function of the goodness of fit between them and the various systems within which they are located and their component relationships; it is a dynamic process characterised by mutual influence and adjustments (Greene and Ephross, 1991; Steiner, 2002). Thus, we have used the term *ecology* to refer to the set of cultural, social and personal circumstances confronting each person as they develop throughout life. According to Steiner (2002, p.2), 'Ecology is, by definition, the reciprocal relationship among all organisms and their biological and physical environments'. The *habitat* is the actual locality in which a person resides and *niche* is the role(s) occupied by that person in an ecological community (Steiner, 2002). In our view, thinking of the cultural, social and personal circumstances as ecological components helps to keep in mind the fact that human beings are *cultural animals* who purposively interact with their environment and develop in a dynamic and interactive manner. Child abuse emerges from a matrix of relationships between individuals, families and their local habitats and niches, and is not simply the consequence of individual psychopathology or problems.

The person's current ecology is also an important contributor to the aetiology of child abuse through making available potential victims, and by creating the specific circumstances (e.g. social alienation, poverty) that trigger any psychological problems involved. This is a proximal dimension; it triggers offending. The ecological niche (social and cultural roles) and habitat of the offender can also be sources of offence-related vulnerability, which in certain circumstances may cause a person to commit an offence in the absence of any significant psychological or family problems. In other words, sometimes the major causal factors resulting in child abuse reside in the ecological niche, not within the person or family. The offending may be quite opportunistic or may be the consequence of circumstances that effectively erode an individual's capacity to behave in an ethical (and typical) manner.

Another important issue concerns the issues of risk assessment and its relationship to the CRM of child protection practice. We will consider the specific risk factors associated with each of the four different aetiological pathways later in this chapter and for now will simply make a few general comments. Risk assessment is concerned with estimating the likelihood of an individual behaving in a harmful way toward themself or others (Little, Axford and Morpeth, 2004). Practitioners typically use clinical judgement, actuarial prediction using specially designed psychological scales, or some combination of these approaches to assess the future risk of an offender. Clinical judgement may, or may not, be rooted in theory depending upon the clinician's knowledge of the field; in the worst-case scenario, it may even be based on idiosyncratic decisions as to which are the most important variables to consider in an assessment of risk. The most commonly employed actuarial risk prediction measures rely almost exclusively on historical or *static* risk factors that cannot change. In the offending area these measures may be previous convictions for past violent offences, an identified lack of long-term intimate relationships and general criminality.

In an attempt to overcome the limitations of purely static actuarial instruments, and to take into account the fact that risk may be reduced by treatment, some researchers have developed classification schemes that additionally incorporate *dynamic* factors: long-term clinical risk factors that are amenable to change (Beech, Fisher and Thornton, 2003). For example, in terms of child sexual abuse, four *stable dynamic* risk areas have been identified:

- deviant sexual interests
- attitudes supportive of sexual assault
- socio-affective problems
- self-management or general self-control problems (Hanson and Harris, 2000).

These have been used to characterise criminogenic need (i.e. they are changeable factors that are related to reoffending: Andrews and Bonta, 1998), as opposed to *static* risk factors that cannot change as they remain in the history of the offender. An even more recent development by Hanson and Harris (2000) is the identification of a number of what they term *acute dynamic* factors. Acute dynamic risk factors are proximal or contextual characteristics which signal the onset of offending. These variables, which can be identified clinically, include evidence of severe emotional disturbance or crisis, hostility, substance abuse and rejection of supervision.

The previous discussion clearly indicates that clinical and empirical perspectives are converging in current notions of risk; research informs clinical judgement and empirically research-driven risk systems are informed by clinical judgement. The state of the art in risk assessment can be seen as consisting of the following assessment components:

1. An analysis of how the abuser's problems contributed to their offending (a functional analysis approach).

2. The application of suitable actuarial risk predictors to assess level of risk (a statistical approach).

3. The identification of psychological problems at the stable-dynamic risk level in order to identify deficits that need to be addressed (a clinical/psychometric approach).

4. The assessment of acute dynamic risk factors that indicate offending is imminent (a monitoring/intelligence approach).

Which combination of these approaches is most appropriate will obviously depend on the characteristics of the offender, the purposes of the assessment and the information potentially available to the clinician or assessor.

In this chapter we attempt to show how the causal pathways identified in the CRM of child protection practice can be mapped onto dynamic risk factors. That is, how the attributes of individuals and poor family functioning can be used to predict whether or not a child is in danger of further abuse. The usefulness of this approach is that it suggests that risk assessment schedules need to be more specifically related to the features of the abusers and families in question. In other words, the cultural and social environment of the family is an essential component driving the practice response. The model also should clarify that the level of risk posed by an abuser is a function of a specific set of causes, and also the context in which these vulnerability factors are activated. But before we go on to discuss the model, we would like to say a word or two about theory and theory development.

The nature of theory in the child protection area

In a nutshell, a *theory* is any description of an unobserved aspect of the world and may consist of a collection of interrelated laws or a systematic set of ideas that set out to explain specific phenomena (Kukla, 2001). *Laws* are true universal propositions referring to all time and space that express causal or necessary relationships among properties. That is, laws spell out what is likely to occur in every situation and across all possible time frames. They are discovered by science. An example of a scientific law is 'All pieces of copper expand when heated'. An example of a possible law in forensic psychology is 'All child molesters have sexual preferences for children'. This is not in fact a law because it is only true for a certain subset of child molesters (Marshall, Anderson and Fernandez, 1999). It should perhaps be qualified in some way and rephrased as a probable law that only applies to those child molesters with certain characteristics. Theoretical terms refer to factors and processes that are unobservable (e.g. intelligence, character traits) while observation terms denote processes that can be directly observed (e.g. test scores, behaviour).

In the child maltreatment area a number of theories have been proposed to account for the sexual and physical abuse of children, including strain theory, social bonding theory, sociological theory and theoretical perspectives (see Miller-Perrin and Perrin, 1999). These theories vary in terms of their level of analysis (e.g. social patterns as opposed to individual psycho-pathology) and their practice utility. All have strengths but individually do not really provide a coherent framework for understanding why individuals abuse children and, related to this, what type of interventions are likely to reduce the risk for reoffending in vulnerable families. Theories are cultural resources available to practitioners and it is our contention that effective practice requires the use of multiple resources from a variety of cultures. We advocate the use of theory blending or knitting techniques to fashion ideas and practices into a supple and effective intervention framework.

Theories of human behaviour set out to achieve two fundamental goals: explanation and prediction (Hooker, 1987; Newton-Smith, 2002). A theory explains phenomena, why they exist and why they possess certain properties. An explanation is basically the application of a theory in order to help understand certain phenomena. It tells a causal story concerning why and how specific events happen and why people behave the way they do. For example, the intimacy deficit model claims that child molesters seek children as intimate partners because they are unable to meet their emotional needs with adults (Marshall *et al.*, 1999). Explanation is *backward* looking; it helps us understand why a particular outcome happened. By way of contrast, prediction is *forward* looking and is concerned with the precise forecasting of outcomes within a system. For example, a researcher might predict that an offender with a dismissive attachment style is more likely than individuals with other attachment styles to behave aggressively toward their victim.

Typically, more than one theory is able to account for the evidence (i.e. under-determination) and therefore empirical adequacy alone does not provide a sufficient basis for deciding between competing theories or even deciding whether or not a theory is worth persevering with. Because of this, theory appraisal has to be undertaken on evaluative dimensions in addition to empirical adequacy. It must be noted that the kind of under-determination we are referring to is transient in nature and is usually resolvable over time (Kitcher, 2001). That is, as two theories are critically compared, a clear winner typically emerges from the testing and evaluation process. A further point is that it sometimes makes sense to develop theories that initially lack empirical adequacy because they are particularly promising in some other respect; for example, because they refer to deep underlying causes (*explanatory depth*) or open up new avenues of inquiry (*heuristic value*).

Because of the issue of under-determination, philosophers have suggested that other criteria-knowledge values (i.e. theory appraisal criteria), such as explanatory depth, coherence and fertility, are equally important for making judgements about which theories to choose from amongst competing theoretical explanations (Hooker, 1987; Newton-Smith, 2002). Knowledge values arguably track truth in some respect. In other words, the set of knowledge values in question, point to a theory's likely truth. Setting aside the question of whether any set of ideas is more or less likely to be 'true', the key idea is that theories exhibiting such values have proved over time to be deeper and more satisfactory explanations; that is, they seem to be giving us a more accurate picture of the world and its workings. Because of this fact, researchers are prepared to argue that the theory in question is more likely to provide this confidence. The following list captures the knowledge values commonly accepted to be good indicators of a theory's 'truth' (Hooker, 1987; Newton-Smith, 2002). 'Truth', of course, is an ideal and unlikely to be achieved. The notion of 'truth' helps us to try and provide a richer understanding of a particular problem. We accept that there can be more than one valid way of explaining a phenomenon, and that perspectives provide unique and valuable insights. Below are the major theory appraisal criteria that help to determine the strength of a set of explanatory ideas:

- *Predictive accuracy, empirical adequacy* and *scope* concerns whether the theory can account for existing findings and the range of phenomena requiring explanation.

- *Internal coherence* refers to whether a theory contains contradictions or logical gaps.

- *External consistency* is concerned with whether the theory in question is consistent with other background theories that are currently accepted.

- *Unifying power* relates to whether existing theory is drawn together in an innovative way and whether the theory can account for phenomena from related domains; does it unify aspects of a domain of research that were previously viewed as separate?

- *Fertility* or *heuristic value* refers to a theory's ability to lead to new predictions and open up new avenues of inquiry. In a practice setting this may also include a theory's capacity to lead to new and effective interventions.

- *Simplicity*, as the name suggests, refers to a theory that makes the fewest theoretical assumptions.

- *Explanatory depth* refers to the theory's ability to describe deep underlying causes and processes.

In summary, the evaluation of a theory or model involves the explicit consideration of a number of different knowledge values (Hooker, 1987; Newton-Smith, 2002). The ability of a theory to account for research findings and to survive hypothesis testing is certainly a necessary requirement for scientific acceptance. Of equal or even greater importance is its ability to extend the scope of existing perspectives and to integrate competing or diverse approaches to the study of the relevant phenomena. In addition, logical consistency, coherence, simplicity and heuristic worth represent important values against which a theory can be evaluated. Ambiguity, inconsistency, vagueness and undue complexity may restrict the overall value of a theory and should be noted whenever they are evident. Theory evaluation is a comparative process and the fact that a theory contains gaps or logical inconsistencies does not mean that it should necessarily be abandoned or rejected. Its value depends on how it compares with other theories in the domain in question.

Levels of theory

Typically, in the few book chapters actually devoted to discussion of child maltreatment theories, theories tend to be classified according to the types of *source* theories utilised in their construction; for example, cognitive, learning, systems, psychodynamic or biological theories (e.g. Miller-Perrin and Perrin, 1999). Thus, researchers talk about psychodynamic theories, learning theory, sociological theories, and so on. In our view this is not the most promising way of categorising theories and results in the confusion of the level of generality (or focus) with the type of psychological systems (e.g. behavioural, cognitive, biological) and theoretical tradition (e.g. psychodynamic as opposed to behavioural). Additionally, theories of the same type (e.g. learning theories) may vary greatly in terms of their breadth and degree of detail. For example, a learning theory framework could be used to explain one type of problem (e.g. attitude supporting violence) or to provide a comprehensive explanation of all aspects of child abuse.

A meta-theoretical framework (a theory about how to create theory!) for classifying theories based on their level of generality of focus, and also upon the extent to which the relevant factors are anchored in both developmental and contemporary experiences and processes, has been provided by Ward and Hudson (1998) in the sexual offending area. In this framework, they distinguished between level I (multi-factorial), level II (single factor) and level III (micro-level or offence process) theories. Level I theories represent comprehensive theories of sexual offending. The aim is to take into account the core features of sexual offenders and to provide a complete account of what causes these phenomena and how they manifest in sexually abusive actions. Level II, or middle-level theories, have been proposed to explain single factors thought to be particularly important in the generation of sexual crimes; for example, the presence of empathy deficits (Marshall *et al.*, 1999). In this approach the various structures and processes constituting the variable of interest are clearly described, and their relationship with each other specified. In a sense, level II theories expand on the factors identified in level I theories. Level III theories are descriptive models of the offence chain or relapse process (e.g. Ward *et al.*, 1995). These micro-models typically specify the cognitive, behavioural, motivational and social factors associated with the occurrence of a sexual offence over time; they constitute dynamic, descriptive theories. The levels of theory model is meant to help researchers distinguish between different types of theory and ultimately to facilitate their integration through a process of *theory knitting*. It is this process that has been most influential in the development of the CRM for child protection practice, and in discussing theory knitting in the context of sexual offending we hope to illustrate a similar development of ideas in child protection theory and practice.

In addition to distinguishing between levels of theory, Ward and Hudson also emphasised the importance of taking into account the distal–proximal distinction. Distal factors constitute vulnerability factors that emerge from both developmental experiences (e.g. sexual abuse) and genetic inheritance (e.g. anxious temperament). These *trait* factors make a person vulnerable to offending sexually once precipitating factors, such as relationship conflict, are present. Although vulnerability factors have their origins in a person's developmental history, they are always causally implicated in the onset of sexually abusive behaviour. For example, deficits in emotional competency may have been acquired during a person's childhood but actively contribute to the onset of sexual offending several years later.

Proximal factors are triggering processes or events, and interact with the vulnerability factors to cause sexual offending. These factors fall naturally into two distinct groups: psychological *state* factors and *situational* events. The state variables are the expression of individuals' underlying vulnerabilities (i.e. the trait or distal factors) and are activated by situational events such as arguments or rejection. For example, emotional deficits are likely to produce powerful negative emotional states in an individual following an argument with a partner or a stressful social event such as losing a job. That is, the person in question may lack the ability to dampen down or communicate their emotions in a healthy way. The negative emotions and the argument or loss of employment are proximal causes that, in conjunction with a person's long-standing difficulties in coping with emotions, directly results in an offence. In this situation, the abuse of a child is used as a means to reduce or control powerful emotions and as such, represents an inappropriate coping response.

Theory knitting

It is useful to blend or knit together theoretical cultures when seeking to improve the power and scope of ideas within a given domain. A theory knitting strategy suggests that researchers can seek to integrate the best existing ideas in an area within a new framework (Ward and Hudson, 1998). This strategy involves identifying the common and unique features of the relevant theories, so it is clear what constitutes a novel contribution and what does not. The major virtue of this approach is that good ideas do not get lost in a continual procession of 'novel' theories that appear briefly in the literature and then disappear forever, often for no good reason.

Kalmar and Sternberg (1988) contrast this perspective with the traditional segregative (where theory development occurs in isolation) approach to the process of theory development in psychology. According to the segregative perspective, different theories are set up in competition and compared for their ability to predict data satisfactorily. Rather than attempting to combine and develop the best elements of each theory, this approach tends to compare individual theories and view them as mutually exclusive and self-sufficient. A major disadvantage of this perspective is that it can trap theorists and practitioners into seeing things only from the point of view of their preferred theory. It can also lead to researchers unknowingly focusing on different aspects of the same phenomenon. The failure to ask 'What can I usefully take from this theory or model?' frequently leads to the premature dismissal of other points of view and the failure to benefit from the resources of other theories.

Outline of the CRM of child protection

The CRM is a multi-factorial model of factors thought to cause child abuse, and a practice model based on this knowledge. It has been 'knitted' together from a variety of theoretical cultures and other forms of cultural thinking including theories and ideas already existing in the child abuse literature; for example, ecological perspectives (Germain, 1991) and problem-solving approaches (Coohy and Braun, 1997). We have also been influenced by the identification of clusters of problems that have frequently been found among adults who abuse children: difficulties in identifying and controlling emotional states; social and relationship problems, and dissatisfaction; cognitive distortions; and physiological or biological difficulties (Coohey and Braun, 1997; Miller-Perrin and Perrin, 1999). Using Lee and Greene's (1999) social constructive framework discussed in Chapter 3, these have been incorporated as abuse-supportive emotions, cognitions and behaviours within the CRM.

We have also drawn from theories of sexual offending; most particularly, Ward and Siegert's pathway theory of child sexual abuse (Ward and Siegert, 2002). The basic idea underpinning the CRM is that intervention in the child protection area needs to be based on the particular set of causes and problems that characterise a family and the individuals concerned. It is a move away from a one-size-fits-all approach where practitioners assume that all cases have the same causes and therefore should be treated in a similar manner. Essentially, we argue that adults may abuse children for markedly different reasons.

The CRM recognises that abusive individuals are likely to vary in terms of the particular profile of clinical phenomena they display. Some abusers may struggle to establish and maintain close personal relationships while others report no problems in this aspect of their lives and instead experience difficulties monitoring their emotional states. In other words, abusers constitute a diverse group who reveal considerable variation in the type, severity and range of problems they present. According to the CRM, the causes of these differences typically reside in distinct psychological causes or social/cultural problems – essentially vulnerability factors.

A key assumption of the CRM is that all abusive actions are the outcome of a number of interacting psychological and social and cultural systems. From a social cognitive perspective, these systems will include motivational/emotional, interpersonal, cognitive and physiological systems (Pennington, 2002). Every human action involves emotions or motives (e.g. the setting of goals), an interpersonal context (e.g. the broader social setting in which actions take place), cognitive interpretation and planning (e.g. the implementation of goals) and physiological arousal and activation (e.g. the physical basis of actions). The different psychological systems are comprised of subsets of causal factors that interact with each other to cause human actions. From the perspective of the CRM, there can be problems in any one of these general systems or their component structures and processes. What this means is that a satisfactory explanation of a complex phenomenon such as child abuse will need to incorporate multiple levels of analysis and specifically address not only its social, interpersonal, emotional, cognitive, biological and physiological dimensions, but also its cultural and systemic dimensions.

A novel feature of the CRM is that all of the problems evident in individuals who abuse children can be organised into four sets of clinical phenomena. Clinical phenomena within the CRM are generated by four distinct and interacting types of social and psychological causes (see Figure 7.1):

- physical and maturational factors
- resourcing factors
- historical factors
- social and cultural factors.

These causes distort the functioning of individuals and the family system, and in effect are usually viewed as *vulnerability* factors. Each of these four sets of causes is hypothesised to impact on the others and their interaction is evident in every episode of child abuse. In other words, every incident of physical abuse of a child will reflect social and cultural factors, physical and maturational factors, resourcing factors and historical factors to some degree. These

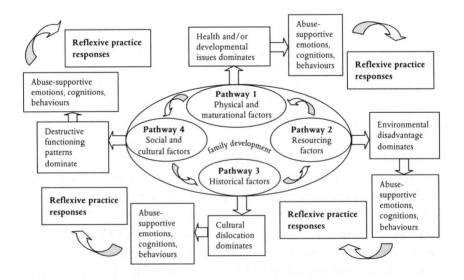

Figure 7.1: Culturally reflexive model of child protection practice (CRM)

variables disrupt the functioning of a family and ultimately combine to result in abuse-supportive emotions, cognitions and behaviours. But according to the CRM, typically one of the four sets of causes is likely to be predominant and in effect drives the abuse by virtue of the emergence of issues that reflect its influence. For example, in one type of child abuse the major cause driving the offence may be identified as resourcing factors and as a consequence the family may experience severe environmental disadvantages such as poverty. The severity and emergence of this underlying problem is jointly affected by the other three types of mechanisms, for example, the health and development of family members, the experience of cultural alienation, and a history of poor parental education and ability to cope with challenging behaviour. However, in this example, the causal factor that constitutes the major problem is poverty and its subsequent effects on the family. The same applies for the other factors: each can function as the primary or driving cause although it is always influenced to some degree by the others, and vice versa.

The dependence of phenomena detection on the information that is gathered emphasises the importance of reliability and validity when collecting information in a practice context. It reminds practitioners to use multiple methods to gather information – relying on just one source, for example self-report, is risky. While self-report is an important source of information, it will inevitably be influenced by the person's view of the world and the possible distorting effects of psychological defences and memory. Under these circumstances professional assessment, if based on self-report, may only capture part of the picture. Thus, it is imperative to ensure that information is gathered in a careful manner and that any errors are minimised as far as it is possible to do so. If assessment scales are used they need to be based on sound psychometric properties. Like any other source of information, however, it is unwise to use them as the only source of information to assess risk. Practitioners need to ask questions in a skilful and structured manner, and ensure that other information sources are available. Expanding areas of inquiry can help to identify bias across the range of interpretations that constitute an abuse investigation. As we noted in Chapter 2, practitioners also need to explore fully the ways in which the information reflects processes of cultural thinking and, indeed, stereotypical notions of what has happened and how.

Abuse pathways

We will now describe a number of aetiological pathways derived from the CRM. It is important to keep in mind that the four pathways to be discussed are not meant to exhaust all possible combinations of causes. They are simply included for illustrative purposes and in a sense represent relatively 'pure' types. According to the CRM, the offence pathways described are associated with different psychological, social and behavioural profiles, each reflecting separate fundamental causes (see Figure 7.1). Each pathway has a distinctive profile in that the relevant primary cause will result in a unique set of problems. The term *primary* is used to mean that the causal factor in question impacts more on other factors than they impact on it; that is, it has more causal influence. In the model, each aetiological pathway has its own unique array of causes that then result in abuse-supportive emotions, cognitions and behaviours. The number and type of cause will vary depending on a pathway's particular developmental trajectory.

Pathway 1: Physical and maturational factors

The major causes in this pathway are related to physical/biological and maturational factors. This area of vulnerability reflects problems with the health of crucial family members and/or marked psychological and social difficulties impacting on developmental functioning of one sort or another. The presence of a developmental problem or illness in a family member creates considerable pressures within a family and in certain situations, can be associated with child abuse. This is particularly relevant when looking at cultures of disability.

For example, if a child is diagnosed with an intellectual disability, the parents may struggle to deal with a number of distinct issues. There is the loss involved with having a child labelled as abnormal, plus the pressure created on the family by the drain on finite emotional and physical resources. If the child in addition is physically disabled, the family's ability to get out and about can be adversely affected and social contact with other families may diminish. This health or developmental issue has the potential to create a parenting culture that may alter the balance of a family's functioning and shift the communication and dynamics from an adaptive to maladaptive pattern. Parents might be asked to take on additional roles, such as paramedical or teaching tasks, and siblings urged to accommodate their brother or sister's needs at the expense of their own. In conjunction with the other three factors, this causal factor may increase the likelihood of child abuse. If a child has a learning or developmental disorder the shame and perceived stigmatisation can result in a family isolating themselves from other families, and defectively cutting themselves off from support, cultural and physical resources. Furthermore, dysfunctional communication patterns in the family, possibly transmitted from one generation to the next, might make it even harder for the parents to express their frustration and also deal competently with their other children's growing resentment of their disabled sibling. In a situation like this, one or more of the parents is likely to believe they have been treated unfairly by the world (interpersonal factors), feel bitter or angry (emotions), see the child as provocative and challenging (abuse-supportive cognitions) and feel unable to ease their escalating levels of stress (physiological). If these factors are sufficiently strong the chances of abuse is heightened.

Reflexive practice responses

The support needs of individuals and families following this pathway reflect the intense pressures of parenting a child with developmental, physical or medical problems. Disability creates a culture of stigmatisation and presents a mixed bag of emotions, expectations and often difficult decisions. Such families need immense support and often specialist services and advice. Critical is the need to explore, understand and work with the culture of disability in the family. How does the disability impact on them as a family? How does it shape their parenting style and how do they understand discipline and control? Simmering resentments and feelings need to be explored, and the way these feelings impact on patterns of family organisation and communication needs to be understood. If the family is isolated their feelings about social isolation and barriers to building their support base need to be investigated. Each family is different. How this family responds to their disabled child and how this impacts on them as a family is essential information if culturally specific plans are to be developed.

Pathway 2: Resourcing factors

In this pathway the functioning of a family is severely compromised by a lack of opportunity to access environmental resources. The kind of resources we have in mind are things such as an adequate income, a good standard of housing, hygienic living conditions, adequate clothing, satisfactory heating, access to basic health care and educational opportunities, and so on. It may also include other environmental constraints such as being geographically isolated and unable to access supports and services that may be available to others. Essentially it results in the family not being able to access the resources they need in order to function well.

The result of a lack of essential resources is likely to be the family struggling to feed, clothe and look after its essential physical needs and, subsequently, high levels of emotional and physical stress. It is anticipated that this factor may interact with the other three primary causes to result in the occurrence of child abuse. For example, a parent in a rurally located family may be unable to find work to support them and their children. The resulting lack of income, partially caused by and interacting with the other three factors, will lead to extreme financial hardship, a lack of adequate resources coming into the family, feelings of parental inadequacy and perceived feelings of disrespect from the children. Previous strategies for controlling children's behaviour may no longer work, impacting on the parent's capacity to deal with the challenges of parenthood and further feelings of inadequacy. They start to feel angry and stressed (emotional problems), believe that their children are being unreasonable and demanding (abuse-supportive cognitions), lack the interpersonal supports and skills to resolve conflicts between them (interpersonal factors) and take refuge in drink, even further reducing the scarce resources available to the family. Their situation is compounded by their relative social isolation and the conservative attitudes to unemployed people in their rural community. These variables combine to create an environment where the threshold for behaving aggressively toward their children is lowered.

Reflexive practice responses

Within this pathway the critical issues revolve around environmental disadvantage, primarily extreme poverty. The parent may be shamed by their inability to find work and this may be impacting on their willingness to seek help either to find work or to access their financial entitlements as an unemployed person. Providing counselling support to address personal inadequacies or offering parenting classes to teach parenting skills, while of general usefulness, is unlikely to resonate with the person's primary problem – the lack of resources to support the family. Unless the worker is able to understand the drivers of abuse the potential for impacting effectively on the abuse-supportive emotions, cognitions and behaviours will be lost. While the parent may have some limitations in terms of managing challenging behaviour, these alone are unlikely to result in the physical abuse of their children. Focusing practice interventions on them is unlikely to result in the hoped-for changes.

Pathway 3: Historical factors

In pathway 3 the major causes are associated with historical factors; for example, the existence of cultural dislocation and its consequential social alienation. The ecological perspective inherent in the CRM suggests that if the match between the values, norms, beliefs and practices of a family and their immediate social and physical environment is poor, they are likely to become socially isolated. In addition, individual family members may suffer decrements in their identity and self-esteem, viewing themselves as unworthy or socially stigmatised. The erosion of cultural and personal identity makes it hard for individuals to pursue their conception of a good life and construct a coherent sense of personal identity, and this lack of a coherent personal identity can lead to wide range of psychological and social problems, for example depression, unhappiness, anger, a sense of meaninglessness and poor family cohesion. For example, the parents in a migrant family may find themselves isolated. They start to feel angry and stressed, and believe that their children are being unreasonable and would behave themselves better if they were back in their home country. They may lack the interpersonal supports and skills to resolve conflicts between them, and their situation is compounded by their relative social isolation and poor English. The children could experience conflict between the cultural expectations in the various domains of their lives; for example, school and the home environment. These variables combine to create a situation where the threshold for the parents behaving aggressively toward their children is lowered.

A related point is that the norms and practices associated with child rearing and family functioning that the family holds could clash with those of the dominant culture, again causing confusion, anger and resentment. It is hypothesised that the three other causal factors may interact with this pathway to produce the kinds of problems evident in cases of child abuse. For example, the experience of cultural dislocation may cause a family to withdraw and become distrustful of social agencies and professionals such as doctors, teachers and government officials. This suspiciousness could mean that the parents fail to apply for all their entitlements, causing them financial hardship. In addition, unresolved family dynamics originating in their country of origin, (e.g. a family dispute) might mean they do not ask their relatives for assistance and this merely compounds their degree of hardship and social estrangement. Finally, the reluctance to utilise medical care could mean that simple illnesses get worse and cause considerable stress and escalating tensions within the family. The parents might feel resentful and angry with the world at large (abuse-supportive emotions), leading them to believe that their children are disloyal to their culture or may be in danger of being disloyal to their parents (abuse-supportive cognitions), encouraging the parents to further socially isolate themselves to protect the family (social factors) and finally becoming increasingly tense and on edge (physiological). The existence of these abuse-supportive problems or phenomena means that the chances of the parents physically abusing their children are significantly increased.

Reflexive practice responses

Within the case study described above there is potential for the social worker to make stereotypical responses in attributing the problems to a particular cultural group's attitudes toward child rearing and ways of controlling children's behaviour. Nevertheless, the critical issues may be more accurately located in the family's cultural dislocation, and unless the worker is able to use cultural resources to engage the family the potential for impacting effectively on the abuse-supportive emotions, cognitions and behaviours will be lost. Alternative approaches have the potential to respond to unique cultural experiences by paying broader attention to cultural dimensions (e.g. family and spiritual well-being) and the engagement of cultural networks and supports. What is important here is to find ways of understanding how the family perceive their situation and to explore the potential for mobilising cultural, community and state resources to reduce the most significant causal mechanism.

Pathway 4: Social and cultural factors

In pathway 4 the major causal factors reside in the family's social functioning, more specifically its tendency to embrace destructive patterns of communication and functioning. This may include the transmission of poor functioning and/or abuse from one generation to another. Psychological and social problems may result such as chronically low self-esteem, poor emotional competence and possibly the maladaptive use of substances (e.g. alcohol) to cope with life problems. In this pathway we hypothesise that individuals who have experienced inadequate parenting as children will find it more difficult to establish stable, intimate relationships when they reach adulthood. In addition, the lack of modelling of appropriate parenting behaviours means that such individuals could lack effective parenting skills. For example, a parent my have been raised within a sexually abusive but strongly religious cultural environment that also fostered harsh punishment regimes in the discipline of children. Children were to be seen but not heard and the dynamics of sexual abuse created isolation for the children in terms of their capacity to access environmental opportunities. This early socialisation may give the parent a sense of entitlement over the child (abuse-supportive cognitions) and may also reduce the capacity of the parent to develop the skills needed to mediate conflict (interpersonal factors). Moreover, because of their own negative developmental experiences, such families may have loose boundaries and diffuse parent/child roles. A final consequence of childhood trauma and adversity in parents following this pathway could be unresolved trauma and an inability to cope with their resulting emotions, thoughts and memories (emotional factors).

It is suggested that the three other areas of vulnerability may interact with this pathway to produce the kinds of problems evident in cases of child abuse. Historical factors relate to the intergenerational nature of abuse and, as already noted above, such dynamics impact on a child's capacity to access environmental resources. Traumatic abuse experiences may make the parent vulnerable to the use of drugs or alcohol to manage their problematic thoughts and feelings, impacting also on their own health and development. The existence of these sets of factors is thought to result in the clinical phenomena associated with child abuse. For example, a history of past sexual abuse may cause the parent to believe that their child enjoys the abuse (abuse-supportive cognitions) and yet feel strong feelings of guilt or anger as it conflicts with their religious beliefs (emotional factors).

Reflexive practice responses

Individuals following this pathway are likely to need a considerable amount of psychological support from helping services. In effect, the primary driver of their abusive behaviour resides in psychological trauma and, related to this, abusive parenting, social and emotional control skills. In these families the culture of abuse needs to be understood and responded to. Of course, responses will differ depending on the nature of abuse. The sexual abuse of children, as discussed in Chapter 6, is a complex culture of offending requiring specialist treatment services and a high degree of vigilance on the part of the worker. Physical abuse manifests a different culture of offending and each situation reveals its own repertoire of cultural thinking that drives the abuse-supportive dynamic. Reflexive cultural practice requires that the worker understands this dynamic and the cultural thinking that drives it.

Evaluation

Clearly any new model needs to be presented cautiously. In building the model we have attempted to harness the strengths of other theoretical explanations and integrate these within a framework of cultural thinking. Having now described the model, we will briefly evaluate its adequacy drawing on the set of knowledge values or theory appraisal criteria described earlier in this chapter: empirical adequacy and scope, external consistency, internal coherence, unifying power, heuristic value, simplicity and explanatory depth. How does the CRM fare when critically set against this established criteria?

In terms of its *empirical scope*, the key issue concerns whether or not the CRM is able to account for the range of child abuse encountered in the child protection area. The four types of aetiological factors generating child abuse situations seem to us to cover the majority of cases likely to come to the attention of social workers and other professionals working with children who have been abused. The CRM was constructed by knitting together factors demonstrated to explain why some situations are likely to result in the abuse of children. The fact that we have integrated four such factors into a comprehensive model suggests it has adequate scope.

By virtue of its ecological orientation, the CRM does have reasonable *external consistency* with theories from other relevant disciplines; for example, systems theory, social and clinical psychology, anthropology and correctional theory. It is able to accommodate the fact that human beings are social, cultural and psychological agents who are embedded in a variety of systems, all of which have an impact on their behaviour and provide a unique contribution to the explanation of child abuse.

With respect to the value of *internal coherence*, the CRM does not appear to suffer from any clear logical contradictions and the various concepts that collectively constitute the theory are mutually reinforcing and cohesive.

The *unifying power* of the CRM within the child protection arena is, we think, extremely promising. It is able to link together different types of child abuse theoretical perspectives (e.g. psychopathological, strain and sociological models) in a coherent and elegant manner. This aspect of the CRM also speaks to its conceptual *simplicity*. In our view it is certainly more complex than a single factor approach to the issue of child abuse but is relatively simple when you take its greater scope and internal structure into account. In other words, it is a relatively simple but not simplistic model that manages to blend a variety of cultural resources into an integrated discourse.

Perhaps the greatest virtue of the CRM resides in its *heuristic value*. We think the fact that the CRM is able to cover a wide range of cases means that it is able to provide sufficient guidance to practitioners working with abusive individuals and distressed families. It reminds child workers that just because there are common features associated with abusive parents or family members does not mean that the causal pathways are the same. This is a real strength of the theory because it encourages practitioners to focus on the primary factors driving a particular offence rather than adopt a one-size-fits-all approach. This degree of specificity is likely to result in better-directed interventions that respond to the particular culture of the family, resulting in less unnecessary stress to families and, we would hope, lowered rates of re-referral.

Finally, does the CRM have good *explanatory depth*? It is important to keep in mind that the CRM is a hybrid model and alongside its ability to account for the different types of abuse it is also designed to guide practice. This feature of the model does mean that it is more general than specific and in this respect it does not have considerable explanatory depth. However, it is not without strengths in this regard. First, its dynamic and multi-systemic nature means that according to the CRM, child abuse occurs for a variety of reasons, with different types of abuse having their own aetiological pathway. Second, the proposal that in any case of child abuse all the four factors are involved, albeit to varying degrees, does give it explanatory power and some depth. Third, the claim that there are four types of phenomena typically evident in every case of child abuse (cognitions, emotions, social factors and physiological processes) is quite novel and useful.

In this chapter we have outlined a reflexive model of child protection practice. We have drawn from theoretical cultures and other cultural resources such as the fields of child abuse, sexual offending, child development, acculturation, geography and ecology, to knit together a practice theory that can account for a wide range of child protection responses. An evaluation of the CRM indicates that it possesses a number of strengths. Our hope is that it will hold enough promise to function as a practice map to guide workers through the incredible complexities of child protection work.

Chapter 8

Final thoughts

We have set out to provide practitioners and researchers with a tool bag of theoretical and practice resources for working across cultures in child care and protection. No doubt many of you will have noted that the resources required are considerable and range over many different content and practice domains. Being a competent child protection practitioner requires the ability to step into a wide variety of cultural environments and demonstrate at least a modicum of skill in all of them. So what we have tried to do in this book is offer some culturally generic ideas that will help workers respond thoughtfully, no matter what culture they step into. We all live out our lives embedded within dynamic and overlapping systems of groups, environments, ideas, norms, values and resources. The fabric of our individual and collective worlds are multi-textured and many coloured. They require us to develop supple and rich practice frameworks.

We hope you will see that children have a special place in this book. Somewhat surprisingly, childhood culture is often invisible in child protection work despite the centrality of their interests. Children approach the world with their own blend of social, cultural, personal and physical resources and are often confused and disoriented when approached within an adult-centred paradigm or culture. We are not saying that children and adults cannot communicate or do not have common ground between them. The terrain overlaps. But the natures of the local landscapes have different features, unique topographies, and the expert topographers are the children themselves.

Families are systems of individuals, each connected to their own array of life worlds and social systems. Families can become distressed and disconnected for a broad range of reasons, each reflecting its own particular history and journey through time. We need to approach individual family situations with humility and openness, and use all the resources at our disposal to detect the fractures and problems that create risk for children.

Offenders seek human goods, as we all do. They are not bad people sadistically seeking to hurt and maim children for the sheer pleasure of it: at least very few do. Their offending behaviour is damaging to children and cannot be condoned. Nevertheless their stories reveal much about the need to foster healthy lives, nurturing family environments and resilient communities. Listening to their stories cautions us against the assumption that there are boundaries to potential.

All human activities and experiences are layered and can be interpreted from a number of viable and valuable points of view. We believe that utilising the vantage points and cultural resources outlined in this book will provide greater opportunities to understand better the nature of cultural thinking and the people we work with. In the end we believe that humans respond to warm and genuine attempts to understand them. The demands of child care and protection work are considerable but the rewards are incalculable. To turn a family around, to protect and give a child a chance to flourish, to become better workers and wiser people, these are the challenges and hopes that light our pathways. We hope that this book contributes positively towards these ends.

References

Anderson, S. A. and Sabatelli, R. M. (2003). *Family interaction. A multigenerational developmental perspective* (3rd edition). Boston, MA: Pearson Education Inc.

Andrews, D. A. and Bonta, J. (1998). *The psychology of criminal conduct* (2nd edition). Cincinnati, OH: Anderson Publishing Co.

Archard, D. W. (2003). *Children, family and the state*. Aldershot: Ashgate.

Arnhart, L. (1998). *Darwinian natural right: The biological ethics of human nature*. Albany, NY: State University of New York Press.

Ashford, J. B., Sales, B. D. and Reid, W. H. (2001). 'Political, legal and professional challenges to treating offenders with special needs'. In J.B. Ashford, B.D. Sales and W.H. Reid (eds) *Treating adult and juvenile offenders with special needs* (pp.31–49). Washington, DC: American Psychological Association.

Aspinwall, L. G. and Staudinger, U. M. (eds) (2003). *A psychology of human strengths: Fundamental questions and future directions for a positive psychology*. Washington, DC: American Psychological Association.

Baldry, S. and Kemmis, J. (1998). 'The quality of child care in one local authority'. *Adoption & Fostering*, 22 (3), 34–41.

Beech, A. R., Fisher, D. D. and Thornton, D. (2003). 'Risk assessment of sex offenders'. *Professional Psychology: Research and Practice*, 34, 339–52.

Belgrave, M. (2004). 'Needs and the state: Evolving social policy in New Zealand history'. In B. Dalley and M. Tennant (eds) *Past judgement: Social policy in New Zealand history* (pp.23–38). Dunedin, NZ: University of Otago Press.

Bell, H. (2003). 'Strengths and secondary trauma in family violence work' [electronic version]. *Social Work*, 48 (4), 513.

Bell, M. and Wilson, K. (2003). 'Introduction'. In M. Bell and K. Wilson (eds) *The practitioner's guide to working with families* (pp.1–15). Houndmills: Palgrave Macmillan.

Benson, C. (2001) *The cultural psychology of self: Place morality and art in human worlds*. Oxford: Routledge.

Berlin, S. B. (2002). *Clinical social work practice: A cognitive-integrative perspective*. New York: Oxford University Press.

Berrick, J. D., Frasch, K. and Fox, A. (2000). 'Assessing children's experiences of out-of-home care: Methodological challenges and opportunities'. *Social Work Research*, 24 (2), 119–27.

Blue-Banning, M., Summers, J. A., Frankland, H., Nelson, L. and Beegle, G. (2004). 'Dimensions of family and professional partnerships: Constructive guidelines for collaboration'. *Exceptional Children*, 70 (2), 167–84.

Blumenfeld, W. J. and Raymond, D. (2000). 'Prejudice and discrimination'. In M. Adams (ed) *Readings for diversity and social justice. An anthology on racism, antisemitism, sexism, heterosexism, ableism and classism* (pp.21–30). New York: Routledge.

Bourdieu, P. (1990). *Language and symbolic power*. Cambridge, UK: Polity Press.

Bourdieu, P. and Wacquant, L. (1992). *An invitation to reflexive sociology*. Chicago, IL: University of Chicago Press.

Braybrooke, D. (1987). *Meeting needs*. Princeton, NJ: Princeton University Press.

Buckley, H. (1999). 'Child protection practice: An ungovernable enterprise?' *The Economic and Social Review*, 30 (1), 21–40.

Carling, A. (2002). 'Family policy, social theory and the state'. In A. Carling, S. Duncan and R. Edwards (eds) *Analysing families: Morality and rationality in policy and practice*. London: Routledge.

Cashmore, J. and O'Brien, A. (2001). 'Facilitating participation of children and young people in care'. *Children Australia*, 26 (4), 10–15.

Cashmore, J. and Paxman, M. (1996). *Wards leaving care: A longitudinal study.* Sydney: Social Policy Research Centre, University of New South Wales.

Charles, M. and Wilton, J. (2004). 'Creativity and constraint in child welfare'. In M. Lymbery and S. Butler (eds) *Social work ideals and practice realities* (pp.179–99). Basingstoke, UK: Palgrave.

Cherlin, A. J. (1992). *Marriage, divorce, remarriage.* Cambridge, MA: Harvard University Press.

Chibnall, S., Dutch, N., Jones-Harden, B., Brown, A., Gourdine, R., Smith, J., *et al.* (2003). *Children of color in the child welfare system: Perspectives from the child welfare community.* London: Department of Health and Human Services. Children's Bureau. Administration for Children and Families.

Cohen, E. P. (2003). 'Framework for culturally competent decision making in child welfare' [electronic version]. *Child Welfare*, 82 (2),143.

Connolly, M. (1999). *Effective participatory practice: Family group conferencing in child protection.* New York: Aldine de Gruyter.

Connolly, M. (2001). 'The art and science of social work'. In M. Connolly (ed), *New Zealand social work: Contexts and practice* (pp.18–31). Auckland NZ: Oxford University Press.

Connolly, M. (2003). 'Cultural components of practice: Reflexive responses to diversity and difference'. In T. Ward, D. R. Laws and S. M. Hudson (eds) *Sexual deviance: Issues and controversies* (pp.103–18). Thousand Oaks, CA: Sage.

Connolly, M. (2004). *Child and family welfare: Statutory responses to children at risk.* Christchurch, NZ: Te Awatea Press.

Coohey, C. and Braun, N. (1997). 'Toward an integrated framework for understanding child physical abuse'. *Child Abuse & Neglect*, 21, 1081–94.

Cooper, B. (2001). 'Constructivism in social work: Towards a participative practice viability'. *British Journal of Social Work*, 31 (5), 721–38.

Crichton-Hill, Y. (2004). 'Assessment with families'. In J. Maidment and R. Eagen (eds) *Practice skills in social work and welfare. More than just common sense* (pp.146–65). Crows Nest: Allen & Unwin.

Cummins, R. A. (1996). 'The domains of life satisfaction: An attempt to order chaos'. *Social Indicators Research*, 38, 303–28.

Dale, P. (2004). '"Like a fish in a bowl": Parents' perceptions of child protection services'. *Child Abuse Review*, 13, 137–57.

Dalley, B. (2004). 'Deep and dark secrets: Government responses to child abuse'. In B. Dalley and M. Tennant (eds) *Past judgement: Social policy in New Zealand history* (pp.175–89). Dunedin: University of Otago Press.

D'Andrade, R. (1995). *The development of cognitive anthropology.* Cambridge, UK: Cambridge University Press.

Davis, A. and Garrett, P. (2004). 'Progressive practice for tough times: Social work, poverty and division in the twenty-first century'. In M. Lymbery and S. Butler (eds) *Social work ideals and practice realities* (pp.13–33). Basingstoke, UK: Palgrave.

Dean, R. G. (2001). 'The myth of cross-cultural competence'. *Families in Society*, 82(6), 623–30.

Deci, E. L. and Ryan, R. M. (2000). 'The "what" and "why" of goal pursuits: Human needs and the self-determination of behavior'. *Psychological Inquiry*, 11, 227–68.

Delfabbro, P. H., Barber, J. G., and Bentham, Y. (2002). 'Children's satisfaction with out-of-home care in South Australia'. *Journal of Adolescence*, 25 (5), 523–33.

DePanfilis, D. (2000). 'How do I match risks to client outcomes?' In H. Dubowitz and D. DePanfilis (eds) *Handbook for child protection practice* (pp.367–72). Thousand Oaks, CA: Sage.

Diller, J. V. (1999). *Cultural diversity: A primer for the human services.* Belmont, CA: Brooks/Cole. Wadsworth.

Diller, J. V. (2004). *Cultural diversity: A primer for the human services.* Belmont, CA: Thomson/Brooks Cole.

Dominelli, L. (2002). *Anti-oppressive social work theory and practice.* Basingstoke, UK: Palgrave Macmillan.

Doolan, M., Nixon, P. and Lawrence, P. (2004). *Growing up in the care of relatives or friends: Delivering best practice for children in family and friends care.* London: Family Rights Group.

Dyche, L. and Zayas, L. H. (1995). 'The value of curiosity and naivety for the cross-cultural psychotherapist'. *Family Process,* 34, 389–99.

Eagleton, T. (2000). *The idea of culture.* Oxford, UK: Blackwell Publishers Ltd.

Eisenhart, M. (2001). 'The meaning of culture in the practice of educational research in the United States and England'. Paper presented at the Symposium Intercultural Research by Educational Anthropologists: Theoretical Perspectives, Geneva, 24–28 September.

Emmons, R. A. (1996). 'Striving and feeling: Personal goals and subjective well-being'. In P. M. Gollwitzer and J. A. Bargh (eds) *The psychology of action: Linking cognition and motivation to behavior* (pp.313–37). New York: Guilford.

Emmons, R. A. (1999). *The psychology of ultimate concerns.* New York: Guilford.

Featherstone, B. (2004). *Family life and family support: A feminist analysis.* Houndmills: Palgrave Macmillan.

Fellin, P. (2000). 'Revisiting multiculturalism in social work'. *Journal of Social Work Education,* 36 (2), 261–78.

Fook, J. (1999). 'Critical reflectivity in education and practice'. In B. Pease and J. Fook (eds) *Transforming social work practice: Postmodern critical perspectives* (pp.195–208). St. Leonards, NSW: Allen & Unwin.

Fook, J. (2002). *Social work: Critical theory and practice.* London: Sage.

Forte, J. A. (1999). 'Culture: The tool-kit metaphor and multicultural social work'. *Families in Society,* 80 (1), 51–62.

Fox, A., Frasch, K. and Berrick, J. D. (2000). *Listening to children in foster care: An empirically based curriculum* [electronic version]. Berkeley, CA: Child Welfare Research Centre.

Franklin, C. (1995). 'Expanding the vision of the social constructionist debates: Creating relevance for practitioners'. *Families in Society,* 76 (7), 395–406.

Freeman, D. (1983). *Margaret Mead and Samoa: The making and unmaking of an anthropological myth.* Cambridge, MA: Harvard University Press.

Freeman, M. D. A. (2000). *Overcoming child abuse: A window on a world problem.* Aldershot, UK: Ashgate.

Garland, D. (2001). *The culture of control: Crime and social order in contemporary society.* Chicago, IL: University of Chicago Press.

Garrett, P. M. (2003). *Remaking social work with children and families: A critical discussion on the 'modernisation' of social care.* New York: Routledge.

Gendreau, P. and Andrews (1990). 'Tertiary prevention: What the meta-analyses of the offender treatment literature tell us about what works'. *Canadian Journal of Criminology,* 32, 173–84.

Germain, V. B. (1991). *Human behaviour in the social environment: An ecological view.* New York: Columbia University Press.

Giddens, A. (1984). *The constitution of society: Outline of the theory of structuration.* Los Angeles, CA: University of California Press.

Gilbert, N. (1997). *Combatting child abuse: International perspectives and trends.* New York: Oxford University Press.

Gilbertson, R. and Barber, J. G. (2002). 'Obstacles to involving children and young people in foster care research' [electronic version]. *Child & Family Social Work,* 7 (4), 253–8.

Gould, N. and Taylor, I. (eds) (1996). *Reflective learning for social work research, theory and practice.* Brookfield, VT: Ashgate.

Greene, R. R. and Ephross, P. H. (1991). *Human behavior theory and social work practice.* New York: Aldine de Gruyter.

Haaven, J. L. and Coleman, E. M. (2000). 'Treatment of the developmentally disabled sex offender'. In D. R. Laws, S. M. Hudson and T. Ward (eds), *Remaking relapse prevention with sex offenders: A sourcebook* (pp.369–88). Thousand Oaks, CA: Sage.

Hanson, R. K. and Harris, A. J. R. (2000). 'Where should we intervene? Dynamic predictors of sexual offence recidivism'. *Criminal Justice and Behavior,* 27, 6–35.

Harker, R. M., Dobel-Ober, D., Lawrence, J., Berridge, D. and Sinclair, R. (2003). 'Who takes care of education? Looked after children's perceptions of support for educational progress'. *Child & Family Social Work*, 8 (2), 89–100.

Hays, P. A. (2001). *Addressing cultural complexities in practice. A framework for clinicians and counsellors.* Washington, DC: American Psychological Association.

Herbert, M. and Harper-Dorton, V. (2002). *Working with children, adolescents and their families* (3rd edition). Chicago, IL: Lyceum Books.

Hetherington, R. (2002). 'Learning from difference: Comparing child welfare systems'. *Partnerships for Children and Families Project.* Retrieved 21 April, 2005, from http://info.wlu.ca/~wwwfsw/cura

Hofstede, G. (1984). *Culture's consequences: International differences in work-related values.* Newbury Park, CA: Sage.

Holland, S. (2000). 'The assessment relationship: interactions between social workers and parents in child protection assessments'. *British Journal of Social Work*, 30 (2), 149–63.

Hollin, C. R. (1999). 'Treatment programs for offenders: Meta-analysis, "what works" and beyond'. *International Journal of Law and Psychiatry*, 22, 361–72.

Holloway, S. L. and Valentine, G. (2000). 'Spatiality and the new social studies of childhood'. *Sociology*, 34 (4), 763–83.

Hooker, C. A. (1987). *A realistic theory of science.* Albany, NY: State University of New York.

Houston, S. (2001). 'Beyond social constructionism: Critical realism and social work'. *British Journal of Social Work*, 31 (6), 845–61.

Hwa-Froelich, D. A. and Vigil, D. C. (2004). 'Three aspects of cultural influence on communication: a literature review'. *Communication Disorders*, 25 (3), 107–18.

Johnson, P. R., Yoken, C. and Voss, R. (1995). 'Family foster care placement: The child's perspective'. *Child Welfare*, 74 (5), 959–74.

Jorgensen, I. S. and Nafstad, H. E. (2004). 'Positive psychology: Historical, philosophical, and epistemological perspectives'. In P. A. Linley and S. Joseph (eds) *Positive psychology in practice* (pp.15–34). New York: John Wiley and Sons.

Kalmar, D. A. and Sternberg, R. J. (1988). 'Theory knitting: An integrative approach to theory development'. *Philosophical Psychology*, 1, 153–70.

Ka Tat Tsang, A. and George, U. (1998). 'Towards an integrated framework for cross-cultural social work practice'. *Canadian Social Work Review*, 15 (1), 73–93.

Kaukinen, C. (2002). 'The help-seeking of women violent crime victims: Findings from the Canadian Violence Against Women Survey'. *The International Journal of Sociology and Social Policy*, 22 (7/8), 5–34.

Kekes, J. (1989). *Moral tradition and individuality.* Princeton, NJ: Princeton University Press.

Keller, J. and McDade, K. (2000). 'Attitudes of low-income parents toward seeking help with parenting: Implications for practice'. *Child Welfare*, 79 (3), 285–312.

Kim, Y.Y. (1994). 'Beyond cultural identity'. *Intercultural Communication Studies*, IV (I), 1–24.

Kim, Y.Y. (2001). *Becoming intercultural: An integrative theory of communication and cross-cultural adaptation.* Thousand Oaks, CA: Sage.

King Keenan, E. (2004). 'From sociocultural categories to socially located relations: Using critical theory in social work practice'. *Families in Society*, 85 (4), 539–48.

Kitcher, P. (2001). *Science, truth, and democracy.* New York: Oxford University Press.

Knutsson, K. E. (1999). *Children: Noble causes or worthy citizens?* Aldershot: Arena.

Koerner, A. F. and Fitzpatrick, M. (2002). 'Toward a theory of family communication'. *Communication Theory*, 12 (1), 70–91.

Korbin, J. E. (1980). 'The cultural context of child abuse and neglect'. *Child Abuse & Neglect*, 4, 3–13.

Korbin, J. E. (1991). 'Cross-cultural perspectives and research directions for the 21st century'. *Child Abuse & Neglect*, 15, 67–77.

Korbin, J. E. (2002). 'Culture and child maltreatment: Cultural competence and beyond'. *Child Abuse & Neglect*, 26, 637–44.

Kroll, B. (1994). *Chasing rainbows: Children, divorce and loss*. London: Russell House Publishing.

Kroll, B. (1995). 'Working with children'. In F. Kaganas, M. King and C. Piper (eds) *Legislating for harmony: Partnership under the Children Act 1989* (pp.88–101). London: Jessica Kingsley Publishers.

Kukla, A. (2001). *Methods of theoretical psychology*. Cambridge, MA: MIT Press.

Lavalette, M. and Cunningham, S. (2002). 'The sociology of childhood'. In B. Goldson, M. Lavalette and J. McKechnie (eds) *Children, welfare and the state*. London: Sage.

Lee, M. (2003). 'A solution-focused approach to cross-cultural clinical social work practice: Utilizing cultural strengths'. *Families in Society*, 84 (3), 385–95.

Lee, M. and Greene, G. J. (1999). 'A social constructivist framework for integrating cross-cultural issues in teaching clinical social work'. *Journal of Social Work Education*, 35 (1), 21–37.

Leigh, J. W. (1998). *Communicating for cultural competence*. Boston, MA: Allyn and Bacon.

Leong, F. T. L. and Wagner, N. M. (1994). 'Cross-cultural counseling supervision: What do we know? What do we need to know?'. *Counselor Education and Supervision*, 34, 117–31.

Linley, P. A. and Joseph, S. (2004). 'Applied positive psychology: A new perspective for professional practice'. In P. A. Linley and S. Joseph (eds) *Positive psychology in practice* (pp.3–12). New York: John Wiley and Sons.

Little, M., Axford, N. and Morpeth, L. (2004). 'Research review: Risk and protection in the context of services for children in need'. *Child and Family Social Work*, 9, 105–17.

Lum, D. (ed) (2003). *Culturally competent practice: A framework for understanding diverse groups and justice issues* (2nd edition). Pacific Grove, CA: Brooks/Cole/Thomson.

Macnamara, J. R. (2004). 'The crucial role of research in multicultural and cross-cultural communication'. *Journal of Communication Management*, 8 (3), 322–34.

Marsh, P. and Crow, G. (1998). *Family group conferences in child welfare*. Oxford: Blackwell Science.

Marshall, W. L., Anderson, D. and Fernandez, Y. (1999). *Cognitive behavioural treatment of sexual offenders*. New York: Wiley.

Maruna, S. (2001). *Making good: How ex-convicts reform and rebuild their lives*. Washington, DC: American Psychological Association.

McGuire, J. and Priestly, P. (1995). 'Reviewing what works: Past, present and future'. In J. McGuire (ed), *What works: Reducing offending – Guidelines from research and practice* (pp.3–34). Chichester: Wiley.

McKee, M. (2003). 'Excavating our frames of mind: The key to dialogue and collaboration' [electronic version]. *Social Work*, 48 (3),401–8.

McLennan, G., Ryan, A. and Spoonley, P. (2004). *Exploring society: Sociology for New Zealand students* (2nd edition). Auckland: Pearson/Prentice Hall.

McPhatter, A. R. (1997). 'Cultural competence in child welfare: What is it? How do we achieve it? What happens without it?' *Child Welfare*, LXXVI (1), 255–78.

Miller-Perrin, C. and Perrin, R. D. (1999). *Child maltreatment: An introduction*. Thousand Oaks, CA: Sage Publications.

Montagu, A. (1997). *Man's most dangerous myth: The fallacy of race* (6th, abridged student, edition). Walnut Creek, CA: AltaMira Press.

Morgen, S. (2001). 'The agency of welfare workers: Negotiating devolution, privatization, and the meaning of self-sufficiency'. *American Anthropologist*, 103 (3), 747–61.

Morrison Van Voorhis, R. (1998). 'Culturally relevant practice: A framework for teaching the psychosocial dynamics of oppression'. *Journal of Social Work Education*, 34 (1), 121–33.

Mossakowski, K. N. (2003). 'Coping with perceived discrimination: Does ethnic identity protect mental health?' *Journal of Health and Social Behaviour*, 44 (3), 318–31.

Mullaly, B. (2002). *Challenging oppression: A critical social work approach*. Toronto, ON: Oxford University Press.

Munford, R. and Sanders, J. (1999). *Supporting families*. Palmerston North, NZ: Dunmore Press.

Munro, E. (1999). 'Common errors of reasoning in child protection work'. *Child Abuse & Neglect*, 23 (8), 745–58.

Munro, E. (2001). 'Empowering looked-after children'. *Child and Family Social Work*, 6, 129–37.

Munro, E. (2002). *Effective child protection*. London: Sage Publications.

Murphy, M. C. (2001). *Natural law and practical rationality*. New York: Cambridge University Press.

Narayan, U. (1999). 'Working together across differences'. In B. R. Compton and B. Galaway (eds) *Social work processes* (6th edition) (pp.243–52). Pacific Grove: Brooks/Cole.

Newton-Smith, W. (2002). *A companion to the philosophy of science*. Oxford: Blackwell.

Nussbaum, M. C. (2000). *Women and human development: The capabilities approach*. New York: Cambridge University Press.

Nussbaum, M. C. (2001). *Upheavals of thought: The intelligence of emotions*. Cambridge, UK: Cambridge University Press.

Ogloff, J. R. O. and Davis, M. R. (2004). 'Advances in offender assessment and rehabilitation: Contributions of the risk-needs-responsivity approach'. *Psychology, Crime, & Law*, 10, 229–42.

O'Hagan, K. (2001). *Cultural competence in the caring professions*. London: Jessica Kingsley Publishers.

Parton, N. (2003). 'Rethinking professional practice: The contributions of social constructionism and the feminist "ethics of care"'. *British Journal of Social Work*, 33 (1), 1–16.

Parton, N. and O'Byrne, P. (2000). 'What do we mean by constructive social work?' *Critical Social Work*. G. B. Angell (ed). Windsor, ON: School of Social Work, University of Windsor.

Parton, N., Thorpe, D. and Wattam, C. (1997). *Child protection: Risk and the moral order*. Basingstoke, UK: Macmillan.

Pease, B. and Fook, J. (1999). 'Postmodern critical theory and emancipatory social work practice'. In B. Pease and J. Fook (eds) *Transforming social work practice: Postmodern critical perspectives* (pp.1–22). St. Leonards, NSW: Allen & Unwin.

Pedersen, P. B. (1991). 'Multiculturalism as a generic approach to counseling'. *Journal of Counseling and Development*, 70 (1), 6–12.

Pennington, B. F. (2002). *The development of psychopathology: Nature and nurture*. New York: Guilford Press.

Pharr, S. (1988). *Homophobia: A weapon of sexism*. Little Rock, AR: Chardon Press.

Rapp, C. A. (1998). *The strengths model: Case management with people suffering from severe and persistent mental illness*. New York: Oxford University Press.

Rasmussen, D. B. (1999). 'Human flourishing and the appeal to human nature'. In E. F. Paul, F. D. Miller and J. Paul (eds) *Human flourishing* (pp.1–43). New York: Cambridge University Press.

Reder, P. and Duncan, S. (2003). 'Understanding communication in child protection networks'. *Child Abuse Review*, 12, 82–100.

Ringel, S. (2001). 'In the shadow of death: Relational paradigms in clinical supervision'. *Clinical Social Work*, 29 (2), 171–9.

Rossiter, A. (1995). 'Teaching social work skills from a critical perspective'. *Canadian Social Work Review*, 9, 627–43.

Saarni, C. (1999). *The development of emotional competence*. New York: Guilford Press.

Saleebey, D. (1992). *The strengths perspective in social work practice*. New York: Longman.

Salmond, A. (2003) *The trial of the cannibal dog: Captain Cook in the south seas*. London: Penguin Books.

Sanders, J. R. (2004). 'Subject child: The everyday experiences of a group of small town Aotearoa/New Zealand children'. PhD thesis, Palmerston North NZ: Massey University.

Schneider, D. J. (2004). *The psychology of stereotyping*. New York: Guilford Press.

Schofield, G. (2001). 'Resilience and family placement: A lifespan perspective'. *Adoption & Fostering*, 25 (3), 6–19.

Schon, D. (1983). *The reflective practitioner*. London: Temple Smith.

Schon, D. (1987). *Educating the reflective practitioner: Towards a new design for teaching and learning in the professions*. San Francisco, CA: Jossey-Bass.

Schonert-Reichl, K. A. and Muller, J. R. (1996). 'Correlates of help-seeking in adolescence'. *Journal of Youth and Adolescence*, 25 (6), 705–31.

Seligman, M. E. P. and Csikszentmihalyi, M. (2000). 'Positive psychology: An introduction'. *American Psychologist*, 55, 5–14.

Sinclair, I., Wilson, K. and Gibbs, I. (2001). '"A life more ordinary": What children want from foster placements'. *Adoption & Fostering*, 25 (4), 17–26.

Smith, A. B., Gollop, M. M., Taylor, N. J. and Atwool, N. R. (1999). *Children in kinship and foster care: A research report*. Dunedin: Children's Issues Centre.

Smith, P. (2001). *Cultural theory: An introduction*. Malden, MA: Blackwell.

Spickard, P. R. (1992). 'The illogic of American racial categories'. In M. Root (ed) *Racially mixed people in America* (pp.12–23). Newbury Park, CA: Sage.

Spillman, L. (2002). 'Introduction: Culture and cultural sociology'. In L. Spillman (ed) *Cultural Sociology* (pp.2–15). Malden, MA: Blackwell Publishers.

Spoonley, P. (1994). 'Racism and ethnicity'. In P. Spoonley, D. Pearson and I. Shirley (eds) *New Zealand Society* (2nd edition, pp.81–97). Palmerston North: Dunmore Press.

Spradley, J. (1994). 'Ethnography and culture'. In J. Spradley and D. McCurdy (eds) *Conformity and conflict: Readings in cultural anthropology* (8th edition). New York: HarperCollins College.

Stangor, C. (2000). *Stereotypes and prejudice*. Philadelphia: Psychology Press.

Steiner, F (2002). *Human ecology: Following nature's lead*. Washington, DC: Island Press.

Stets, J. E. and Burke, J. (2000). 'Identity theory and social identity theory'. *Social Psychology Quarterly*, 63 (3), 224–37.

Swidler, A. (1986). 'Culture in action: Symbols and strategies'. *American Sociological Review*, 51, 273–86.

Tajfel, H. (1978). *Differentiation between social groups: Studies in the psychology of intergroup relations*. London: Academic Press.

Taylor, C. and White, S. (2000). *Practising reflexivity in health and welfare: Making knowledge*. Buckingham, UK: Open University Press.

Thomas, N. and O'Kane, C. (1999). 'Experiences of decision-making in middle childhood: The example of children "looked after" by local authorities'. *Childhood*, 6 (3), 369–89.

Thomas, N. and O'Kane, C. (2000). 'Discovering what children think: Connections between research and practice'. *British Journal of Social Work*, 30, 819–35.

Thomson, G. (1987). *Needs*. London: Routledge and Kegan Paul.

Thompson, N. and British Association of Social Workers (2001). *Anti-discriminatory practice* (3rd edition). Basingstoke: Palgrave.

Toews, J. E. (1998). 'Having and being: The evolution of Freud's Oedipus theory as a moral fable'. In M. S. Roth (ed) *Freud: Conflict and culture*. New York: Knopf.

Wacquant, L. (1998). 'Pierre Bourdieu'. In R. Stones (ed) *Key sociological thinkers*. New York: New York University Press.

Walker, P. (2001). *The fox boy: The story of an abducted child*. London: Bloomsbury.

Walmsley, C. (2004). 'Talking about the aboriginal community: Child protection practitioners' views'. *First Peoples Child & Family Review*, 1 (1), 63–71.

Ward, T. (2000). 'Happy birthday...goodbye!'. *Social Work Now*, 17, 21–7.

Ward, T. and Hudson, S. M. (1998). 'The construction and development of theory in the sexual offending area: A meta-theoretical framework'. *Sexual Abuse: A Journal of Research and Treatment*, 10, 47–63.

Ward, T. and Siegert, R. J. (2002). 'Toward and comprehensive theory of child sexual abuse: A theory knitting perspective'. *Psychology, Crime, & Law*, 9, 319–51.

Ward, T. and Stewart, C. A. (2003a). 'The treatment of sex offenders: Risk management and good lives'. *Professional Psychology: Research and Practice*, 34, 353–60.

Ward, T. and Stewart, C. A. (2003b). 'Criminogenic needs and human needs: A theoretical model'. *Psychological, Crime, & Law*, 9, 125–43.

Ward, T., Louden, K., Hudson, S. M. and Marshall, W. L. (1995). 'A descriptive model of the offence chain for child molesters'. *Journal of Interpersonal Violence*, 10, 452–72.

Weedon, C. (1987). *Feminist practice and poststructuralist theory*. Oxford: Basil Blackwell.

Weick, A. and Saleebey, D. (1995). 'Supporting family strengths: Orienting policy and practice toward the 21st century'. *Families in Society*, 76 (3), 141–9.

Williams, C. C. (2004). 'Race (and gender and class) and child custody: Theorizing intersections in two Canadian court cases'. *NWSA Journal*, 16 (2), 46–69.

Williams, R. (1976). *Keywords: A vocabulary of culture and society*. London: Fontana.

Wilson, L. and Conroy, J. (1999). 'Satisfaction of children in out-of-home care'. *Child Welfare*, LXXVIII (1), 53–69.

Wise, S. (2003). *Family structure, child outcomes and environmental mediators: An overview of the development in diverse families study*. Melbourne: Australian Institute of Family Studies.

Woodcock, J. (2003). 'The social work assessment of parenting: An exploration'. *British Journal of Social Work*, 33 (1), 87–106.

Worden, M. (2003). *Family therapy basics* (3rd edition). Pacific Grove: Thomson. Brooks/Cole.

Yates, D. (2001). 'Sink or swim: Leaving care in New Zealand', *Social Policy Journal of New Zealand*, 16, 155–73.

Yee Lee, M. (2003). 'A solution-focused approach to cross-cultural clinical social work practice: Utilizing cultural strengths'. *Families in Society*, 84 (3), 385–95.

Zastrow, C. H. and Kirst-Ashman, K. K. (2004). *Understanding human behavior and the social environment* (6th edition). Belmont, CA: Thomson. Brooks/Cole.

Zeldin, T. (1994). *An intimate history of humanity*. London: Minerva.

Zink, T., Elder, N. and Jacobson, J. (2003). 'How children affect the mother/victim's process in intimate partner violence'. *Archives of Pediatrics & Adolescent Medicine*, 157 (6), 587–5.

Subject index

abuse *see* child abuse; child sexual abuse
African-American families 25–6
agency *see* personal agency
anthropology 17
Aristotle on good lives 98
assessment 82, 83, 119
     see also risk assessment
assumptions *see* stereotyping
authoritarian/ authoritative parenting 81

beliefs *see* cultural identity; tacit cultural knowledge
bias *see* prejudice; stereotyping
birth families *see* families
black and ethnic minorities *see* ethnic minorities

care, children in *see* looked after children
child abuse
     aetiology 105–6, 107–11, 114–16, 117–19
          historical factors in 118, 119, 123–4
          physical and maturational factors in 118, 119, 120–1
          resourcing factors in 25, 118, 119, 121–2
          social and cultural factors in 118, 119, 124–5
     definitions 23–4, 25
     inquiries 44
     see also child sexual abuse; intergenerational abuse; sexual offending
child-centred practice 71–3
child protection
     and culture 22–5, 35
     help-seeking approaches 54, 55–6, 80
     and social constructivism *see* social constructivism
     theory 111–12
          evaluation of 112–14, 116
          levels of 114–16
          theory knitting 115, 116
          under-determination in 112
     tools for 45–7
     work with children 70–3

see also child abuse; culturally reflexive model; culturally responsive practice
child protection system
     characteristics 35, 43
     development of 44–5
     ethnic minorities in 25–6
     see also service development; supervision
child protection workers *see* practitioners
child-rearing practices, cultural differences 24–5
child sexual abuse
     risk factors 110, 124–5
     see also sexual offending
children
     adult perceptions 59–60
     listening to 61–2, 64–5, 70–1
     sociological studies 61–2
     working with 70–3
     see also looked after children
communication
     and assessment 82
     with families 78–9, 82
     and power relationships 81
     see also meaning; supervision
connectedness in the supervision model 85, 87–8
constructivism 47–8
     see also social constructivism
criminogenic needs and treatment choices 94–5, 96, 104
critical reflection 37, 38–42
cultural awareness
     of practitioners 26–8, 31, 48–50
     see also stereotyping
cultural environment
     and cultural identity 51, 100
     dislocation of *see* historical factors
     and sexual offender rehabilitation 102
     see also ecological perspective
cultural identity 19–20
     and communication 78–9
     and cultural environment 51, 100
     external/ internal variables 50–2
     practitioners' awareness 26, 31, 49–50
     and problem perception and solution 52–5
     and psychological well-being 99
     and supervision 84–9
     see also tacit cultural knowledge
cultural knowledge 27–8, 30–1, 39

cultural literacy 27
cultural reflexivity
     family violence, perspective on 34
     and the personal self 31–3, 37–8
     process 36–42
     and the professional self 33–7, 38–42
     see also critical reflection; culturally reflexive model; culturally responsive practice
culturally reflexive model 107–11, 116–18
     evaluation 126–7
     historical factors in 118, 119, 123–4
     physical and maturational factors in 118, 119, 120–1
     practice responses 34, 121, 122, 124, 125
     resourcing factors in 118, 119, 121–2
     social and cultural factors in 118, 119, 124–5
culturally responsive practice
     and child protection tools 45–7
     with children 71–3
     with families 79–84, 87
     training in 46–7
     see also cultural reflexivity; problem perception and solution; social constructivism; supervision
culture
     and child protection 22–5, 35
     concept 15–18, 32–3, 92
     in offender rehabilitation 92–3
     see also family cultures; social and cultural factors
cultures, theoretical 33–5

decision making, children's participation in 64–5
difference in the supervision model 85, 86
disability 40, 51–2, 121
     see also physical and maturational factors
discrimination *see* exclusivity; prejudice; stereotyping
distal factors in sexual offending 115
domestic violence *see* family violence
domination *see* oppression; power

Author index